暗室之后

等候着她的

光明之王

**O magnify the Lord with me, and
let us exalt His Name together**

To

Dr. Frank and Mrs. Lucille Toney:

May the Lord, Jesus Christ, Whom we love and serve together bless you both, and may your united lives be a blessing to many.

Christiana Isai.

(Bedridden for 32 years.)

Paradise,
Penna,
January 5,
1963.

QUEEN OF THE DARK CHAMBER

The Story
of
CHRISTIANA TSAI

As told to
ELLEN L. DRUMMOND

Drawings by
ELLEN L. DRUMMOND

MOODY PRESS
CHICAGO

Library of Congress Catalog Card Number 53-3854

First Printing, August, 1953

Second Printing, October, 1953

Third Printing, February, 1954

Fourth Printing, September, 1954

Fifth Printing, January, 1955

Sixth Printing, September, 1956

Seventh Printing, October, 1956

Eighth Printing, February, 1957

Ninth Printing, July, 1957

Tenth Printing, May, 1958

Eleventh Printing, June, 1958

Twelfth Printing, March, 1959

Thirteenth Printing, November, 1960

Fourteenth Printing, October, 1961

Fifteenth Printing, April, 1962

Sixteenth Printing, December, 1962

Printed in the United States of America

DEDICATED

TO

MY LOVING GODMOTHER

MISS MARY A. LEAMAN

WHO LED ME

TO

THE ROAD OF PEACE

ALONG WHICH WE HAVE WALKED

TOGETHER FOR OVER

FORTY-FIVE YEARS

A Personal Recommendation

of

QUEEN OF THE DARK CHAMBER

Because the Spirit of God breathes through its pages I am glad to commend *Queen of the Dark Chamber* to Christian readers everywhere.

It witnesses to the adequacy of Christ in these crucial times. It emits the fragrance of faith in a world so polluted with the stench of sin. It demonstrates unmistakably that faith in Christ triumphs over every vicissitude and unfavorable circumstance of life. The blight of disease, the pangs of persecution, and the darkness of illiteracy flee before His power as darkness flees from the radiance of the noonday sun.

The author has made us feel the heartbeat of a nation and has done much to interpret the sufficiency of Christ to a great and needy people. In her furnace of affliction Miss Tsai has discovered the secret of spiritual refining. In her dark chamber of infirmity she has found the Light of the World.

May her testimony, her work, and her challenge as presented in this book enjoy wide reading and ready acceptance. May thousands of her people discover the Radiance which has kept her heart aglow, even in the Dark Chamber of suffering.

BILLY GRAHAM

4

Foreword

*T*HE VERY NAME Christiana reminds us of the pilgrim in Bunyan's immortal allegory. More than that, the life story of Christiana Tsai depicts the unusual experiences in the pilgrim pathway of a Chinese believer. The facts presented in this autobiography are truly stranger than fiction. How marvelous that in early girlhood Christiana, though the daughter of a wealthy Confucian official, should meet the Lord and respond to His claim! Her mind and heart were early impressed with the divine declaration, "I am the way, the truth, and the life." Not only did Christiana appropriate this truth for herself, but she devoted her life to the making known of the One whom she recognized as Saviour of the world and the hope of her nation. Thus Christiana became a pilgrim of The Splendid Way.

As you see how through her the light-giving and life-giving power of the Gospel of Christ is made known, there will come a fresh realization of the infinite value of foreign missions. For Christiana is truly the fruit of missionary endeavor. Through the transformation of this life, scores within her own large family and clan were brought to know her Saviour. Through Christiana's work and the promotion and translation of the Scriptures in phonetic script, hundreds have come to an experience of God's saving grace; thousands of humble believers have learned to read God's Word and to form Bible-reading habits.

Miss Mary Leaman and Christiana Tsai worked as colleagues in this monumental work of preparing the translations of the Scriptures in phonetic script. Their lifelong partnership in service for Christ and the people of China is a beautiful example of loving co-operation between Oriental and Occidental. Who can evaluate all that has been accomplished for Christ and His Kingdom by the sacrificial efforts of these devoted servants of the Lord?

Perhaps it should be explained that the percentage of the Chinese people, even among Christians, who are able to read their national language is comparatively small. This is not to be wondered at when one considers the thousands of ideographs and the years of schooling necessary for the acquisition of this difficult written language. The reduction of countless ideographs to thirty-seven phonetic symbols enables unschooled folk, even country women, after a few weeks of assistance in classwork, to read the Scriptures. As a result of the help of the phonetic script, many have acquired a working knowledge of the national language.

It is a privilege to commend the reading of this autobiography. It is Christiana's desire that the Lord who called her receive the glory through this record of her life. Many have been blessed through Miss Tsai's ministry. May many more be blessed through her testimony.

HERBERT M. GRIFFIN
Director for North America,
China Inland Mission,
Philadelphia, Pa.

Preface

Most girls in the Orient have no first name. As we read the life of our Lord Jesus Christ, we become acquainted with the names of the brothers in His earthly family, but we are amazed when we realize the sisters are not named (Matthew 13:55, 56). This fact was, and still is, true in China especially in the countryside.

Although Sister Seven has a very beautiful name, she is known to her family and relatives only as Sister Seven. Because of their background, the people of the Orient understand the Bible perhaps better than those of the West; and the quotations from Scripture used in this inspiring story are very adequate, because the author knows from Chinese culture, as well as personal experience, their real interpretation.

The only hope of the world today is our Lord Jesus Christ. There is no other hope. American dollars cannot save the world, no matter how many we have. Atomic bombs cannot conquer the world, no matter how powerful they are. Salvation lies in the redemptive love of our Lord Jesus Christ. How shall we lead more men and women to know Christ, and to live Christ? Many reasons and excuses are given for our failure to do this. If you are excusing yourself, read this story and feel ashamed.

Sister Seven has been in bed for twenty-two years, yet her Christian life is one of radiance, and of such joy and trust that she has led many souls to Christ. The best way to preach Christ is by our daily life. The greatest joy in life is to experience a change of heart, through the power of the Holy Spirit, and become a follower of our Lord. A true sign of a real Christian is the peace and joy experienced, despite pain and difficulties in our everyday life. This story will stir your heart.

Once a great scholar in China said, "A sage seeks opportunities in difficulties, and a fool finds difficulties in opportunities." After reading this story you will find the author is a sage. We are born to overcome difficulties through the power of the Holy Spirit. What can we do for God in this time of difficulty and uncertainty? You will find the answers in this inspiring story. Read it carefully.

The last four months I have spent making a survey of all the Chinese Christian churches in this country, including the Territory of Hawaii. Everywhere I go people ask: "What can I do for China?"

My survey revealed over one hundred thousand Chinese in this country, but only about ten per cent of them Christians. The door to China is tightly closed today. Shall we not rather ask, "What can we do for the Chinese people here among us?" Let us accept the challenge and show not only an interest in their land, but in them as a people. Some day, many of them will return to China as doctors, nurses, social workers, teachers, mechanics, and above all, evangelists and missionaries. If America is faithful in these her days of opportunities, what a help and strength these folk will be, when the door is again opened, and they go home, with a vital personal experience with our Lord, to become leaders in all avenues of life!

Strangely enough, some people in this country do not believe in missionary work. But if this book could be placed in their hands, I am sure the Holy Spirit would open their eyes and never again would they doubt the value of work accomplished through consecrated lives.

Personally I will recommend this moving story to our ministers and members of our seventy-one Chinese churches in the U.S.A., and also I will encourage my personal friends among other churches to read it. I count it a great honor and joy to have been privileged to read this story and write the Preface. I am sure God will use it to save many souls, and to stimulate the interests of many young people to become missionaries.

In addition to the spiritual value of this moving story, it is also a good source book for Chinese family life. Most books on China are written by Westerners. Sister Seven is a native, from a wealthy, cultured and scholarly home. You get a true picture of Chinese family life; and it would be especially good for use in a missionary study group.

Above all, it is a devotional book. Before I wrote this Preface I shared this story with our staff members and our young people, and they were more than pleased to read it. They all felt the power of the Holy Spirit as they read of this saint of God, who has so fully yielded her life to the Master, and is being so wonderfully used of Him. We covet a wide circulation for this book, that it may become known to the many who need the transforming power of the Holy Spirit; and that it may challenge Christians to a deeper consecration.

> REV. PETER Y. F. SHIH, S. T. M., D.D.
> Director of the Chinese Mission of New England.
> Pastor of The Chinese Christian Church of New England
> 54 Harvard Street, Boston 11, Mass.

Acknowledgment

It is a pleasure to acknowledge with thanksgiving the kind and sacrificial help of an old China friend,

Miss Ellen L. Drummond

for her patient attention to my story and her careful writing. Her knowledge of the background, and acquaintance with most of the people, have been invaluable, and her drawings are true to the life and times described.

Christiana Tsai

Contents

I Want You to Know

I want you to know you are never forgotten,
  The Saviour is with you, He sees all your grief;
Remember, He cares, He will never forsake you,
  And soon He is coming to bring you relief.

I think of you daily and pray for you always,
  How often I see you in darkness and pain;
But tho' you must suffer, His grace is sufficient,
  And some day with Jesus forever you'll reign.

The Lord will be with you, dear Queen of the darkness,
  And all of earth's shadows will soon pass away;
For you have been faithful and many in Heaven
  Will praise you for turning their darkness to day.

Your book has brought blessing, it makes me unworthy,
  For you have accomplished so much by His grace;
Some day you will step from your chamber of darkness,
  For Jesus remembers; you'll see His dear face.

With Christian affection, my sister from China,
  I send you this message—your pray'rs He will hear;
I want you to know that God's mercy is o'er you,—
  Forgotten? no, never! your Saviour is near.

—OSWALD J. SMITH

To Christiana Tsai,
Queen of the Dark Chamber.

I have seen the vision
And for self I cannot live;
Life is less than worthless
Till my all I give.
    —O. J. S.

Illustrations

CHAPTER I

The School of Adversity

IT WAS THE TWELFTH DAY of the second month, and all over China, people were celebrating the Birthday of the Flowers, by tying red strips of cloth on the trees and bushes. These red strips fluttering gaily in the breeze were their birthday greetings to the new flowers.

My father, however, had no time for such celebrations. He was busy at his desk in the Viceroy's Yamen* when a servant entered and saluted him, "Great Master, I have good news to report. You have a new daughter and the madam is well."

"Another daughter!" my father sighed. "That makes eighteen children in all. Too many! Too many!"

"Too Many" became my baby name. Though their first greeting was not enthusiastic, my parents did not neglect me. They sent around the customary red eggs to all our relatives and friends to tell them of my arrival. When I was one month old, these relatives and friends came to visit me, bringing gifts of embroidered caps, baby shoes, bibs and similar articles. Then they enjoyed a feast including a dish of chicken noodle soup. Noodles are a symbol of long life, and are always served on birthdays.

In spite of the fact that my parents thought eighteen children were too many, erelong another sister arrived, and they gave her the baby name of "Full House." She was followed by number twenty, who was also a sister, so they called her "Running Over." All my sisters were good-looking, but I was considered rather

*Governor's administration building.

plain. Yet it was I, alone, "Too Many," who left the high ancestral walls to enter a mission school, crossed the ocean to America, and now have the honor of writing to you.

Hangchow, near the coast of central China, is my old family home. Here the Tsai family have lived for generations and here are the graves of my ancestors. Hangchow is one of the beauty spots of China, famed for its flowering hills, picturesque West Lake, historic temples, storied pagodas and the swift-flowing Chientang River that sweeps its southern walls and then empties into the long narrow neck of the Hangchow Bay. There the river crashes into the high spring and fall tides as they surge in, forming a wave of foaming water which advances for miles back up the river, submerges both banks along the way. This phenomenon is called the Hangchow Bore. So great is the beauty of Hangchow that there is a common saying, "Heaven is above; Hangchow and Soochow are below."

My grandfather was born in the early part of the nineteenth century, when the Manchu emperors still ruled China. After he passed the government examinations required for a high literary degree, he received an appointment to the governorship of the important Province of Kwangtung, in the south. So he left his wife, six sons and a daughter in Hangchow, and made the long journey south to take up his new post. Alas, no sooner had he reached it than he was stricken with disease and died. When my grandmother heard the news, she was stunned. She sat like a statue for days. Her sons tried in vain to move her, get her to speak, eat, or go to bed. She only sat staring in front of her. Now with no visible means of support, she must raise six sons and a daughter. She, who had been trained to ease, must toil night and day. She must dismiss the servants, sell the house, and pawn all the fine garments. Her family must learn to eat rice gruel and cabbage. But she resolved, come what may, all her sons would be scholars, in the family tradition.

My father was the second son, and many a time he told us of

Three children in old-fashioned clothes

his childhood poverty. "How do you think I got my education?" he would ask my brothers, when they complained of hard work. "We did not even have a teacher or the books we needed. I had to walk through wind and swirling snow for miles to borrow a book, and agree to return it after a certain number of days. Then we boys, after a day's hard work, would sit together around the table and copy from the borrowed book. In the center of the table was a small cup of oil, with a floating wick, giving a very dim light. When we were hungry we would eat a handful of cold, leftover rice from the basket. In the winter months our hands were so numb we could hardly hold our pens. You don't know what hardship is!"

Somehow the family managed to get along. The boys were largely self-educated, the elder taught the younger. When they grew to manhood, they prepared to take the literary examinations that opened the way for civil service, just as their father and grandfather had done. The daughter, of course, was not allowed to study. She was only a girl and must learn to do the housework.

My father and his older brother passed the first degree examinations in Hangchow, and later went to Nanking to take the examinations for the next degree. On the day appointed, the two brothers appeared at the Examination Halls. Both were dressed in long blue cotton gowns and short black coats. Their hair was neatly braided in long queues and they wore black skull caps; each carried a basket containing fruit, pens, ink, a bowl and chopsticks.

Gaily colored awnings hung over the entrance. At the gate two attendants roughly searched the young men for hidden papers or books. They entered an open courtyard where crowds of students and attendants milled around. A high tower overlooked the many long rows of examination cells which extended on four sides from the tower. Each row contained about a hundred cells, opening into a narrow aisle, and exposed to the weather in front.

The two brothers were very nervous and kept close together to bolster their courage. They were assigned separate cells where they laid down their baskets. The cells were the size of telephone booths, and each contained a narrow board to sit on, a niche in the wall for a light, a nail to hang the basket, and another board for a table.

Soon the examiners summoned them to the courtyard, called the roll and gave each student his roll of paper. This was all the paper he was allowed, so he carefully hid it in the pocket of his gown. Toward evening, the examiners went to the street gates and with great ceremony closed and sealed them. This was a signal that the examinations were to begin. For three days and nights no one could go out or come in for any reason whatever.

In the tower overhead, an examiner appeared and beat a gong to call the students to assemble in the courtyard. They gazed up and saw him wave a banner. He called out in a loud voice: "O ye spirits of the dead! Look upon these students gathered here! If

Examination cells and tower

any has offended you in word or deed do you now punish the offender and avenge the wrong." The nervous students, who believed in evil spirits, shivered with fear, some nearly fainting. The gong was sounded again, and the students went to their own cells.

An attendant, holding a lighted lantern with the subject of the essay written on the sides, passed slowly down each aisle, giving the students time to see the title clearly. During the three days and nights, the students could neither lie down to sleep or speak to anyone; an attendant paced up and down the aisle to guard against any cheating.

At mealtimes when the gong sounded, each took his bowl and chopsticks out to the courtyard, where there were great steaming caldrons of rice gruel. He dipped out what he wanted, noisily wolfed it down, and then turned back to the cell. The strain of preparation, anticipation and prolonged concentration was so great that there were always a few students who died under the ordeal, and their bodies were passed out through a secret door in the wall.

When the essay was finished, each signed his name on the designated flap, sealed it and handed the paper to the examiner. Then when the gates were opened, they went out, too weary to speak, anxious only for a place to lie down for a few hours. The examinations were strictly impartial. The subjects always demanded thorough knowledge of Confucian Classics. The Board of Examiners read each essay and judged it on its own merits before they unsealed the author's signature. Appointments were often given to those who received the highest grades. This system of examinations had been in operation in China since A.D. 600.

One day a messenger handed an official notice to my grandmother stating that my father had passed the examination! Grandmother had no money to give the messenger for bringing the good news, so she took her best coat to a neighbor for a deposit, and borrowed money. She and Father were very happy, but my uncle was so disappointed he went to his room and wept. Soon another messenger arrived with a notice saying that uncle too had passed.

Another coat was taken to the neighbors, and more money borrowed to pay the second messenger, and the family sat down to celebrate the great occasion, shabby but proud.

Every member of the family eventually won an important political post. My eldest uncle became Vice-Governor of Hopei Province, living at Tientsin; and my father Vice-Governor of Kiangsu, living at Nanking. Later he became Acting-Governor, and held many other important offices. My third uncle became a high official (*Taotai*) in Peking; my fourth uncle, Mayor of Paotingfu; my fifth uncle, Mayor of Yangchow; and my sixth uncle, Mayor of Siangyang, in Hupeh. As for the despised little girl, she married an official having the highest rank of all, instructor of the Emperor himself! Such are the sweet uses of adversity!

Many years later my father became head of the Examination Halls in Nanking. He used to don his gorgeous robes, put on his cap with a peacock feather hanging down behind and a red button on top (the insignia of the highest official degree), and set out in his green sedan chair with eight bearers. Liveried horsemen preceded and followed him.

Father always had a deep affection for the poor and did much for them. One night during the examinations he decided to see what was going on below. He took off his official robes, put on an attendant's gown and went downstairs. In the darkness of the courtyard he heard someone sobbing. He found a student huddled on a step, crying as if his heart would break. "What is the matter?" Father asked. "Who are you?"

"My name is Hung, and I am from Wusih. My widowed mother is too poor to send me here, but some friends loaned money for me to come. My essay slipped out of my gown and fell into the night soil! Alas, now I have no more paper and I dare not return and tell my mother I have lost the chance! It would break her heart! I can only kill myself." My father was moved with compassion. "I have a roll of paper which I do not need," he said. "I will get it for you, and you can rewrite your essay. Wait

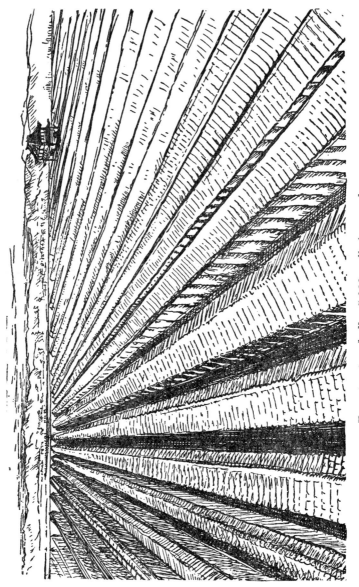

Examination halls—5,000 cells for students

here for me." When he returned the young man looked in his face, recognized him as the Chief Examiner and kowtowed before him. "Sir," he cried, "I shall remember you with gratitude all my life. You have saved me and my mother!"

The next incident after passing his examinations was a strange marriage. In China engagements are often made when both parties are young, and arranged without either the boy or girl seeing each other. Sometimes the parents arrange them even before the children are born. So it happened that at an early age my father was engaged to a young woman whom he had never seen and who lived far to the north, in Peking. As there were no mails in those days, and they had had no news of her for some years, my grandmother urged him to go up to Peking, marry his bride, and bring her home.

The journey to Peking took several months and was very tiresome and difficult. He was surprised to find on arrival that she had been dead two years, and her coffin was there waiting for him! According to Chinese custom, she was his wife and he must bring her coffin back to Hangchow and bury her in his family graveyard. Now his first wife was dead, so he must marry again. He married a girl from Hangchow who bore him seven children and then she too died. After her death he went to Peking again and married a beautiful young lady, with whom he fell deeply in love. This woman, my mother, was not only beautiful, but very capable and a great help to him in his work. She was slender, with delicate features, and an ivory-tinted complexion. Her jet black hair was brushed smoothly back into a knot at the neck, and fastened with gold and jade hairpins. She bore him fifteen children. But her burdens as wife and mother, and mistress of a vast household, were so great, that she urged my father to take a concubine to share the responsibilities with her. The latter bore him two children, so in all he had twenty-four children,—quite a family, even in China, where big families are common.

After my father had had various political offices, and had been stationed in several cities, he went to Nanking, where he lived from 1870 to 1910.

CHAPTER II

Inside High Walls

*P*EKING, "Northern Capital," lies in the dusty plains of North China. Within its high walls the Manchu Empress Dowager lived in indescribable splendor, ruling over her vast empire. Nanking, "Southern Capital," lies in the green fields and hills of the Yangtse Valley and has been the political trouble spot in Central China. After the Manchus were overthrown, Nanking served as capital under various governments during the last half century. It lies on the southern banks of the Yangtse, about two hundred miles from its mouth. Its lofty city walls curve with the natural contours of the land, enclosing an immense city area, while its nine city gates with their storied towers look down on the stream of burdened coolies, creaking wheelbarrows, speeding ricksha men, battered carriages and gleaming cars passing through its portals. Each conveyance pictures in a way the kaleidoscopic events that these ancient walls have witnessed in recent times.

It was in Nanking that I was born, seventh in line of daughters, and so was called "Miss Seven." Who could have dreamed that I was to see Nanking throw off the yellow Manchu gown, put on a Republican suit, then change to a Japanese uniform, and later go back again to the Republican outfit?

It was through these city gates that my father passed in his green sedan chair as Vice-Governor of the Province of Kiangsu. It was outside these walls, in a little houseboat, that the pioneer missionaries waited until they could find a home to live in. In their wake came an ever growing stream of missionaries. The

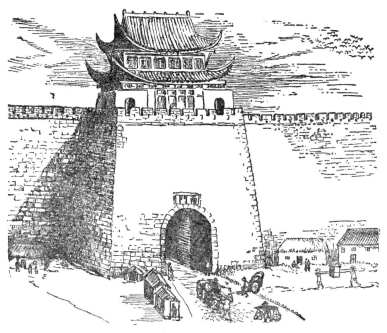

A city gate

churches, schools, seminaries, colleges, hospitals, and homes scattered over the city are material evidence of their devoted work, while the changed lives and society around them continue to show the enduring spiritual results. From the river and the hills around the revolutionaries besieged the city in 1911 and drove out the Manchus, opening the way for Sun Yat Sen, father of the Chinese Republic, to come in as the first president of China. Through these same gates, sixteen years later, Chiang Kai-shek entered and made Nanking his capital. In 1937, after only ten years of this rule, a Japanese army blasted a corner of the wall, entered the city, raping, burning, and looting with great ferocity. The Japanese were defeated eight years later, and Chiang Kai-shek re-entered the gates of Nanking.

How well I remember our home on the Street of the King's Favorite! It was an amazing labyrinth of halls, courtyards, dwellings and gardens surrounded by high walls. Let me take you there. We will enter an imposing gateway flanked by stone lions, pass through brass-studded lacquered doors, on each side of which are long benches where the retainers sit, and find ourselves in a courtyard that opens into a lofty hall. The hall is furnished in stiff, carved tables and chairs, and the walls are hung with immense scrolls. Passing through a door at the back, we find ourselves in another courtyard, with still another hall back of that. But there are two doorways set on either side of the courtyard and we will enter one of these which is quaintly shaped like a round moon. Inside is a beautiful hall with scarlet and gold pillars, latticed doors, delicately painted ceiling, and carved rosewood furniture. Here we find Father interviewing a guest. When he wants to dismiss the guest, he merely raises his teacup, and the retainers call out, "The guest is leaving."

So from courtyard to hall we wander, from surprise to fresh surprise. Here is a garden with pavilion and climbing roses. There is a library where my brother is reading a book. Next we come to a pond with a rockery and weeping willows, where some children are playing and watching the yuan-yang ducks swimming around. Beyond is a gaily painted theatre where we have plays on special occasions, and next to that a lotus pond with an overhanging balcony where we will drink tea and eat nuts. Each doorway is a different shape—a moon, a leaf, a fan, a vase. Each window set in the wall is a different design of tiles. Everywhere are flowering trees and plants.

If we turn in another direction, we will come upon the living apartments of the family. Most of them are in rows of seven rooms with latticed doors, but we must enter from the middle room, which is the family hall. In front is a square table with stools around it where some children are eating breakfast. On each side of the hall are bedrooms. The beds are immense canopied structures of polished wood inlaid with mother-of-pearl and neatly piled with brightly colored quilts.

Each of these halls and gardens had a special name such as,

He raises his cup and the servants call, "the guest is leaving."

Ancestral Hall, Wisteria Arbor, Magnolia Study, White Crane Pagoda, Bamboo Grove, Fairy Fox Pavilion, etc.

And now let me introduce you to my family.

During my early childhood, there were still eight unmarried children at home. Each of us had two special servants, and one of them always accompanied us wherever we went. The nurse stayed with the child for at least three years and was a mother to him. My nurse stayed with me for sixteen years, and we were devoted to each other.

One important item of etiquette for Chinese children is to learn to speak politely to others, especially to their elders. Instead of saying "Good Morning" or "Good Night," or "Good-by," we addressed people simply by their titles, such as "Father," "Mother," "Great Elder Brother," "Second Elder Brother," "Sixth Younger Sister," "Great Uncle," "Second Sister-in-law," etc. We were never allowed to use our given names for each other as this was not considered polite. So for practice I had to go around and address the animals, "Sister Cat," "Brother Dog," and "Brother Horse." We had two men teachers for the boys, and two women teachers for the girls, a music teacher and a sewing teacher. Because my father wanted us to know Chinese history, he employed two storytellers to instruct us.

Foot-binding for girls began when they were six years of age. Though Father had forbidden it, Mother was practical and knew that society still considered it necessary for every well-born girl to have bound feet if she were to get a husband. She ordered that my feet be bound, but my nurse took pity on my tears and at night often loosened the bandages and gently rubbed my feet. So my feet didn't become smaller and smaller every year as my elder sisters' did, and on New Year's Day I was not allowed to wear embroidered red shoes. "Look at your big boats!" my mother cried. "You'll never get married; you can wear only black shoes."

Eight of my brothers were married and their wives and children lived with us, each in a separate apartment with their own servants. My married sisters, of course, went to live with their husbands' families. Then there were about twenty cousins, children of my uncles, living with us. The men cousins were married and lived with their families and servants in their own apartments. Each of the sisters-in-law and cousins-in-law had her own maid to comb her hair, attend to her wardrobe and to her various needs.

In the kitchen there was a head cook with fifteen assistants who served meals to each family in their own quarters. They fed all the servants as well, for these servants all lived within our walls in rooms assigned to them. There was a head gardener with his assistants, and there was an apartment especially for tailors who did all our sewing. There were many chair-bearers and grooms for the horses. At night two watchmen went about beating drums, and two king thieves were paid to keep other thieves away. They always frightened us at night by leaping up on the roofs and whistling to warn other thieves that they were there. In charge of these were head-servants who had their own assistants, and a treasurer who paid the bills. Mother was in charge of all,—sons, daughters, daughters-in-law, nieces-in-law, grandchildren and servants. The head servants reported to her and she gave orders through them. She had to administer all the discipline and keep order in this great family. The secret of her success was that though she exacted formal obedience, she gave each family freedom to live their own lives in privacy and according to their own desires.

Every morning after breakfast each son and daughter, daughter-in-law and cousin went to the apartment of Father and Mother to address them. They simply said, "Father! Mother!" and then went away unless they received some special orders.

Father was a tall, thin man who was always solemn and dignified. Every evening when he returned home in his green sedan chair, liveried servants would line up on both sides of the main entrance, holding up bright-colored lanterns. As he stepped out of the chair, a servant preceded him to the private entrance calling, "The great one has arrived." That was the signal for us children to line up and address him, and he always acknowledged our salutations with a nod. Little Jade, the concubine, then came forward, took off his embroidered official gown, and put on a garment suitable for the house. We children seldom saw him except on these formal occasions.

Dressed up for the New Year

CHAPTER III

Golden Days

CHINA NEW YEAR was the happiest time of the year for us children. But it was also a great ordeal because we were afraid of committing an error in etiquette and being reprimanded. We believed that all the countless ceremonies must be carried out punctiliously if we were to have good luck throughout the year—any slip might bring bad luck. At least a month in advance the servants began cleaning the house from top to bottom, and preparing great quantities of food. There is a saying in China, "Whether you are rich or poor, you must all scrub and be clean to greet the New Year."

A week before New Year, some of the adults gathered in the kitchen to send the Kitchen God to Heaven. A picture of him was pasted on the wall of the kitchen all year, and he was supposed to watch over the family doings. They kowtowed and burnt incense and placed an offering of candy before him, after which the picture was torn down and burned. We believed that the candy would give him a sweet taste in his mouth, and hoped that he would report only good things about us when he got to Heaven.

By New Year's Eve all preparations had to be complete and all debts paid. Good wishes were written on wide strips of red paper and pasted on the doors. Everyone bathed and put on his new clothes. The men all had queues in those days, and they wore black skull caps and fur-lined, satin gowns. The women and children wore short fur-lined or padded silk jackets, and red embroidered skirts and shoes. The women wore velvet or satin head bands, encrusted with pearls or jade ornaments, to keep their ears

31

warm, and we children wore tasseled caps and silver lockets. We each carried a little covered brass stove containing a red-hot charcoal brickett hid in ashes, to keep our hands and feet warm; for our houses were not heated.

After Father and Mother had given each of us gifts of money to put under our pillows for good luck, we all went to the Ancestral Hall to worship our ancestors. Paintings of our ancestors hung on the walls, and before each picture was a bowl, a cup, chopsticks and a spoon for that person's spirit to use. Long tables were covered with steaming food—whole roast pigs, ducks, chickens, fish, and so on—offerings for the spirits. We all knelt in order of rank and kowtowed, after which the servants brought yellow bags of paper money, one for each ancestor, and gave them to Father, who burned them one by one in a great brass urn, and threw a cupful of wine on the ashes in farewell. When the ceremony was over we all went to the great hall for the feast. We seldom slept at all on New Year's Eve. In the morning of the New Year the doors were all opened, a barrage of firecrackers set off, and we were free to do what we liked for eighteen days, except that we must still worship our ancestors each day of that period.

Every New Year we called in a fortuneteller to "calculate our fortunes" for the year. Blind people generally become fortunetellers because the Chinese say that since they cannot see this world they must be able to see the unseen world. The fortuneteller was led in by a little boy, and he carried a sounding brass disk which he tapped as he went along. He calculated our fortunes on the basis of eight characters—the year, the month, the day and the hour of birth. Chinese calculate time in cycles of sixty years, and each cycle is subdivided into periods of twelve years, each of which is called after an animal. I was born in the year of the tiger, the twelfth day of the second month, at ten o'clock at night. Since I was born in the year of the tiger at night time, and a tiger goes out to hunt prey at night, the fortuneteller said I would be diligent and never lack for food, but girls born on the twelfth day of the second month, the birthday of the flowers, turn out to be either the very best or the very worst among women. So they are not likely to get married. A man's family would rather take the chance of avoiding a wicked wife than of getting a paragon.

With such a fortune, Mother was never able to contract an engagement for me. When I was a few years old, a wealthy family from a city in the north sent a go-between to our homes to seek an engagement for one of their sons. She described the advantages of marrying into that family, and my mother inquired from other sources concerning them. After several months of talking back and forth, Mother agreed to match our fortunes and handed my eight characters written on red paper to the go-between. She took it to the boy's family and they called in a fortuneteller to see whether his eight characters and mine would portend a happy marriage. Since they couldn't be sure which way I would turn out, they decided not to contract the engagement. Had that part of the procedure been fortuitous, the next step would have been to place our eight character strips together under the incense burner which stood before his ancestral tablets for a period of three days. If no misfortune occurred to the family during that time, that is, if nothing were broken, not even a bowl or a chopstick, they would know that I would never break his good fortune and our marriage would be propitious. Once an engagement is agreed upon, the boy's eight characters and those of the girl are written in special red and gold folders. Possession of these folders is equivalent to having a marriage license.

These foolish superstitions reveal how slender is the thread of happiness that binds two lives together, and how blindly people grope in the face of the unknown future to escape the tragedies that lurk beside their pathway. In fact, we Chinese have a proverb that though a bride may ride in a red embroidered sedan chair, she may have picked up an unlucky ticket after all. But this incident also shows that a loving heavenly Father guards His child in all circumstances, working all things together for good, and using even a blind fortuneteller's prognostications for my advantage.

In the ninth month, when chrysanthemums were at their

height, the gardener arranged hundreds of pots in geometric designs beside the garden walks and inside the Colored Glass Hall, before the whole family—father, mother, children, sisters-in-law, cousins, their wives, and grandchildren—all dressed for the occasion met together to celebrate the Chrysanthemum Festival. No one can appreciate the beauty of these flowers who hasn't seen the great varieties of color, size and form that can be grown. We first walked around enjoying them while the servants set chairs and carved teapoys among the pots. Then we sat down, each to his own teapoy, and ate steamed crabs. Everyone had a board, tiny hammer, a pick and a hook to crack the shell and extract the delicious meat. In the meantime, the cook was busy at a great caldron of boiling soup. Into it he dropped bits of fish, chicken, mushrooms, leeks, cabbage, water cress and other delicacies. Finally he put in a bowlful of pure white chrysanthemum petals. We all had a drink of this broth called "Chrysanthemum Pot."

When the eating was over, we all sat in silence while each one composed a short poem for the occasion. We read them in turn, and Father awarded the honors. Seventh Brother and Sixth Sister were generally the best poets; I never even got honorable mention. In this way we carried out the ancient tradition of Chinese poets.

Of course, there were other festivals during the year, but most of the time we either played in the gardens or studied with our teachers, for Father wanted his daughters also to be educated. The lotus pond was big enough to have a little boat, and with a servant to pole us around, we could pick the lotus flowers and eat the seeds from the lotus pods. My brothers had horse races in the big orchard, while we girls hid in the Buddhist temple and watched excitedly. We enjoyed the Hall of Western Culture where there were strange upholstered leather chairs on casters, and we thought it was great fun to roll them around the room. We never thought of sitting on them, for we hardly considered them chairs.

We lived in a fabulous fairyland and beautiful and costly things were given to us, but we were rarely allowed outside the high walls. Prisoners in the palace we dreamed of the world outside. Going to a school just for girls, where a foreign woman would teach me English and piano was my castle in the air.

But there was one day in a year when the doors were opened for us, and our eager eyes drank in the magic sights and sounds of the outside world.

There was an amusement place by the Confucian Temple, in the south part of the city, where we enjoyed an excursion once every summer. For nights before, I hardly slept. In the morning of the great day I dressed in my summer silks and jewelry, and stepping into a sedan chair curtained with silk gauze, went to the shore of a famous canal skirting the temple grounds. Here my father had hired two immense pleasure boats, amazing affairs with fancy railings and carved windows. We all got on these boats and were poled back and forth in the widest part of the canal. The cooks and servants followed in smaller boats with the food, for this was a day of great feasting. First they served us appetizers, tea and soup with tiny meat balls, steamed dumplings, spring rolls, ham and nut biscuits, date and nut cookies, and the like. At noon we had a real feast, with a first course of eight cold dishes, such as minced ham, sliced duck, smoked fish, alkaline eggs. Then followed six hot dishes, brought in one at a time, such as shrimp and peas, shredded pork and bamboo shoots, liver and water chestnuts. Next followed hot dishes such as bird's nest soup, sharks' fins, eight-precious-fruit pudding, and last of all, four huge platters with a whole roast duck, a whole stewed chicken, a whole large fish, and a big roast of pork. Of course, we took only a nibble from each plate and barely touched the last course.

Dinner lasted about two hours, and while we were eating, dozens of singing girls came on to dance and sing for us, magicians did their tricks, and there was a Punch and Judy show. In the afternoon we children climbed into small boats and were poled down the canal to a large peach orchard, where we could pick all the peaches we wanted. In later years, there was a foreign style restaurant where we went in the evening, to eat foreign food. The menu always consisted of beef soup, meat sandwiches, cold sausage, pudding, cocoa, bread, butter and jam. This was nothing short of marvelous to us, but we didn't dare touch the knives or forks for fear of cutting our mouths, so we ate everything with a large spoon. We were also entranced by a foreign shop in the restaurant where we could buy leather pocketbooks, tiny bottles of perfume, and jars of hard candy.

When my mother was forty years of age we had a double ceremony, celebrating her birthday and Third Brother's marriage to the granddaughter of Li Hung-chang, a well-known ambassador to the United States. Troups of noted actors were hired to perform in our private theatre continuously for three days. Three days before the wedding the bride's trousseau arrived, carried by many servants. Chairs, tables, stools, tubs, cradles, chests, cupboards, trunks, boxes, rolls of silk, satin, velvet and tapestry, jewelry, porcelainware, kitchenware, silver, scrolls, vases and screens, formed a procession over a mile long. As each servant with his article came to our entrance, eight of our secretaries stood on each side of the gateway to receive him. Those on one side called the name of the article, and those on the other checked the item on their list. Then the articles were taken to the bride and groom's apartments, and we had to pay a fabulous sum in tips.

On the day of the wedding, all the doors were opened from the brass-studded ones on the street, to the last hall at the back; all screens were removed, allowing a view from the front clear to the back. Archways of bamboo, festooned with green and scarlet silk streamers, were erected. At the front entrance were two rows of our tallest menservants, dressed in long official gowns, their chests crossed with scarlet and green sashes. Beyond the servants, my brothers and cousins stood in a double line to welcome the men guests. Farther in, my sisters and sisters-in-law stood to welcome the women.

When a man guest arrived, his chair-bearers set him down at the entrance, and one of our servants came forward to receive his big red calling card. Then, holding this card high over his head with one hand, he led the guest down the aisle to the men of the family, who greeted him before he was taken to the theatre and seated with the other guests. When a woman guest arrived, her chair was carried on past the men to where the women of the family greeted her and had her escorted to an upstairs balcony of the theatre, where the women watched the play through bamboo curtains.

Late in the day, after all the lanterns were lighted, we heard the trumpets and knew that the great, red bridal sedan-chair was arriving. But, strange to say, the gates were shut and barred, and no one was there to welcome her. The bearers had to set the chair down while the bride's relatives paid a big sum to our servants to open the doors and let her in. This little device was supposed to teach her patience in her new home. When the doors were opened, her chair was brought to the front hall, where the groom stood to welcome her. At the same moment, an ear-spliting barrage of firecrackers was set off. Her two bridesmaids pulled back the curtains, and she stepped out in her elaborately embroided scarlet and green satin gown, heavy pearl-encrusted headdress and veil. The bride and groom now bowed together to heaven and earth, and next bowed to each other, after which the groom went with the bride to the bridal apartment and removed her veil.

From there the couple went to the big hall where the whole family stood to welcome the bride before escorting the couple to the Ancestral Hall where everyone kowtowed before the ancestral tablets. The bride and groom next kowtowed to Father and Mother, and then in turn to the rest of us, from the eldest to the youngest. Returning to the bridal chamber they sat together on the bed behind an embroidered curtain, and exchanged cups of wine. There was a big feast for the guests who teased the bride.

Father and Mother and the other elders each gave the bride an expensive gift, and she in turn gave separate gifts to every member of the family, and money to each of the servants. The cost of weddings and funerals has put many a family in debt for life.

CHAPTER IV

Roots of Bitterness

OUR HOME on the Street of the King's Favorite was a small-scale copy of the sumptuous summer palace of the Manchus in Peking. We were Chinese and, though we didn't know it, were living in the twilight of the Manchu dynasty. These rulers had conquered China in 1644 and forced the Chinese to wear the queue as a sign of subjection. Then they followed the invariable course of tyrants; after establishing a mighty empire, they gave themselves up to enjoying the luxuries they had squeezed from the poor. A brilliant, crafty old woman, the Empress Dowager, sat on the Dragon Throne at Peking. She had gained her power by devious means and held tenaciously to the old order of things. So, while the court rioted in splendor in the palace, the common people, in despair, began rioting in the country, in an effort to overthrow their foreign rulers. The Manchu and Chinese officials were blindly self-satisfied and abysmally ignorant of the Western world, so they resisted all efforts to establish trade and diplomatic relations with the West.

England, France and America coveted the vast potential trade of China and were determined to exploit her resources. Unfortunately, in the case of England, they forced the sale of opium on China. When one of the Chinese officials, a Mr. Ling, resisted by burning a whole cargo of opium, the English backed up their demands with gunboats, won the so-called "Opium War," and demanded important treaty ports with extraterritorial privileges as indemnity. So the progressive West won the diplomatic, military and economic victories over the reactionary East, and reduced the Chinese nation to political impotence, and embittered the whole country for generations to come. Though the Empress Dowager was largely responsible for these defeats, the people, resentful of all foreigners, frequently rioted in an effort to drive them out, not only the Manchus but also the Westerners.

Kwang Hsu was the young heir to the Manchu throne, and he was an enlightened liberal who had the real good of the nation at heart. His wise advisers had helped him prepare a program of reform. The Empress Dowager opposed this, so they plotted to dethrone her. One of the conspirators turned traitor and went to the Empress while she was sitting in the theatre and whispered the details of the plot in her ear. There in the sight of all she listened and her face never moved a muscle. She gave orders to imprison Kwang Hsu. So the last effort to reform the government was nipped in the bud: Kwang Hsu remained a prisoner for life and the Empress Dowager triumphed for a time.

All over China there was increasing resentment against foreigners. Pioneer missionaries suffered much persecution during those years. The Chinese people had long ago organized in mutual protection societies to avenge their wrongs. The Green Society generally used peaceable means, but the Red Society used violence. The Red had greater power over northern China, and the Green in southern China. The Red Society, the Big Sword Society, and the Boxer Society were all similar organizations. They became the media through which the common people expressed their resentment of their oppressors, whether native, Manchu, or Western.

My father was charitable and loved the poor. At the end of every month we used to see a line of poor widows, each holding a receipt book, coming to receive their monthly support. On the hot summer days he ordered two five-gallon jars of fresh tea to be placed in front of our street door, for use of the tired passers-by. He provided free medicine for travelers who became ill. On windy, snowy nights, groups of servants would be sent out to look for the poor in different parts of the city and give them rice tickets and tickets for a set of winter clothes. When a poor person was sick and had no money to see a doctor, or died without money to buy a coffin, my parents encouraged us children to take out our savings, or New Year's money, to help them.

My father was a liberal, and a conscientious leader as well. He sternly forbad Mother to accept any bribes whatsoever. When he had to decide the fate of any man, whether to condemn him to death or set him free, he often spent the whole night pacing up and down in his study. He was friendly to Westerners and risked his life to save them. He later lost his fortune in unsound investments by listening to the advice of some Europeans.

Charles Leaman, the first Protestant missionary to buy land and establish work in Nanking, arrived in 1874. He wore Chinese clothes and had his hair braided into a queue. But since the Chinese always seized a man by his queue, Mr. Leaman had it cut off and attached to his cap. He carried his money, consisting of pieces of silver, sewed into the lining of his sleeveless jacket, which he wore inside his long gown. When he needed some money, he would take a penknife, slit open the jacket, take out a piece, weigh it, and purchase what he needed. At the change of the seasons, he pawned his old garment to buy a new one. He could find no place to rent in Nanking, for the people were afraid of foreigners. He had to sleep wherever he could find a corner, and eat the food of the common people. During the day he sat in the teashops and talked with the men who came to drink tea and discuss their various affairs. Three times a day he went out on the streets to preach. Foreigners were so little known here that the people thought he was a Chinese from the coast.

He married Miss Lucy Crouch, a South China missionary, also of the Presbyterian Church. They went to Nanking where they carried on a pioneer work and devised means to get land for a chapel and a home. Magistrates were unwilling to sell or rent to foreigners, so in the meantime, Mr. and Mrs. Leaman and their little daughter Mary spent many months living in a small houseboat on the canal outside the city walls.

Christiana Tsai

*Christiana's
Mother*

*Tsai Garden
and Christiana's
Watchtower*

*Tsai Home
Inner Entrance*

*Mary Leaman
Proof-reading
the Phonetic Bible*

Miss Tsai seated, is handing her sun glasses to Miss Leaman. Miss Leaman's sister is on her right, and her cousin is on her left.

Finally they bought some land, a former battle ground, which the Chinese considered unlucky for they thought it was haunted by the spirits of the dead. "If you want this land," the magistrate had said, "you can go and live with the devils there." Here they built two houses, a church, and a school. More missionaries arrived, and a third house was built. This was the beginning of the first Presbyterian mission station at Four Flagstaffs.

Mrs. Leaman had been a teacher in Canton's well-known True Light School, which was founded by her dear friend, Miss Noyes. She had studied the far-reaching possibilities of a truly Christian girls' school, and longed to start one in Nanking. Boys in China often got an education, but girls rarely learned to read. Here in Nanking, neither the girls nor their parents saw the value of a woman learning to read, so they were not interested in going to school when Mrs. Leaman advertised. For three months no girl dared enter the compound, then one day a little girl came in. Mrs. Leaman let her play around for the first few days so she would get used to things, and then suggested they start learning to read. The girl refused immediately, saying, "I only came to eat and play; I don't want to study!" And she went away.

The next pupil was the gateman's daughter, and she had to be paid to study! No one at that time would have dreamed that in the lifetime of the Leaman's two daughters, Mary and Lucy, the school would have an enrollment of sixteen hundred students! Nor did anyone foresee that there would soon be dozens of girls' schools right in Nanking. Often in recent years I have seen the students of this school, in celebration of Founder's Day, dramatize those early days. It was very real to them, but at the same time from their sophisticated point of view, very amusing!

There were a number of riots against foreigners in those early years. The people feared and hated the "foreign devils," and spread many rumors about them. One day they seized Mr. Leaman, bound him with ropes, and were going to throw him into a canal. Friends ran to tell Mrs. Leaman. Carrying baby Lucy, and leading Mary, she arrived at the scene just in time to save him. Another mob, led by members of the Big Sword Society, decided to kill the foreigners one night. As they marched toward the Leaman home, rattling their great swords, a big storm came up and they were delayed. Christian Chinese friends warned the Leamans, who hurriedly got into sedan chairs and escaped through the back door, just as the rioters rushed in the front way.

In the meantime, the wily Empress Dowager, hoping to save herself from the rebels, had persuaded the Boxer Society that the Westerners were the cause of China's troubles. She incited them to start a nationwide anti-foreign, anti-Christian massacre. All foreigners in the country were to be killed. Bands of Boxers tortured and murdered both foreign and Chinese Christians. My uncle, Mayor of Pao-ting-fu, died just at this time, and there was a terrible massacre in that city. Forty-six missionaries were killed in one day! Many years later I stood on the very spot where they died, facing their graves. A prominent American speaker read to the group a letter written by one of them to her son in America, just before she died. She told him of their suffering and danger, and yet urged him to prepare and come to China as a missionary to take up their work after they were gone. "And now," said the speaker, "that boy is on his way to China." That was the true spirit of Christ who prayed for His enemies while He was hanging on the cross.

In Nanking, Father received the Empress' order to kill all the foreigners in his jurisdiction. He was acting-viceroy while the viceroy was absent, and knowing that his superior also opposed this order, he decided to disobey it. He changed the words "kill all foreigners" to "protect all foreigners." This was a dangerous step to take, for if his insubordination had been discovered, he and all his family would have been killed. Then he came home and told Mother, "I will not kill these innocent people, and we may all be killed for disobeying the Empress' order. You must take the whole family and go hide in the country." When word of this was passed around, everybody began to weep, until Mother said, "That would be impossible! What could I do alone with this big family on my hands?" In the end we did not run away, and all the foreigners and Christians were spared in our area. We, too, were safe, as the Empress Dowager never received word of Father's insubordination; an international army captured Peking at this time, and she herself was forced to flee.

CHAPTER V

The Deceitfulness of Riches

*T*O AN UNTHINKING PERSON, this picture of wealth and ease would mean that our family was very happy. But underneath the peaceful life was a feeling of pessimism. We knew by experience the vanity of life and the deceitfulness of riches. For Father, who made it all possible, it was the success of a self-made man, trained in the school of adversity. From childhood he had developed his power by hard work, and in later years the money we spent had been acquired, not by corruption in office, but by honest business investments.

We children, cradled in luxury, had nothing to do but enjoy his wealth. We had no incentive for hard work, wherein we might have found some happiness and strength; we became haughty, wasteful, and idle. My elder brothers especially, used Father's money in gambling, carousing and loose living. My sisters, who had married into wealthy, influential families, often came home in tears, complaining of their cruel mothers-in-law and selfish sisters-in-law. Many of the family smoked opium and our rooms reeked with its sickening sweet smell. Once when I was in severe pain, my sister brought me an opium tray and urged me to smoke. Though at other times I had refused, I yielded once. But the sudden way in which the pain stopped warned me there would be danger if I repeated this panacea, so I determined never to touch it again. Many opium smokers first contract the habit in order to relieve pain, only to find that they are later powerless to break away.

Third Brother was the worst profligate in the family. He

loved to dress in flashy clothes and ride fine horses. If a groom offended him, instead of dismissing the man, he sent him to the magistrate for a public beating, until my father put a stop to that. Since he dared not invite his companions to our home, he would steal out at night. When Father set a man to watch before his door, Brother climbed through a side window and got away. In the morning, when the guard opened the door, he found the curtains of the bed closed and shoes beside the bed, but when he looked inside, it was empty.

Since Father now refused him more money, Brother devised tricks to secure it. One day he went to a goldsmith's shop where Mother traded, and told them she had sent him to buy six gold bracelets and charge them to her account. The owner knew his bad reputation and suspected that this was a trick, so he sent a clerk home with him to collect the money. Arriving at the door, Third Brother smoothly told the clerk to wait at the entrance till he got the money from Mother. The clerk waited all day, but Brother never showed up. Finally the clerk told the gateman to inform Mother why he was waiting. Mother got the message and sent for Brother. Needless to say he had taken the bracelets out a back door, pawned them, and had already spent the money. When Father heard this he was beside himself with rage, and picking up a big knife, rushed to Brother's apartment, seized him by the queue and threatened to kill him. Mother heard the noise, rushed in screaming and seized Father by his queue. The servants heard the confusion, and came in and separated the three.

One of my sisters had married the son of an even wealthier official, whose residence was like a king's palace. This official was a libertine who had accumulated his wealth by taking bribes. He had twelve beautiful concubines to each of whom he gave an extravagantly furnished apartment, but no matter how late the hour, these concubines could not close their doors and retire until he had placed the signal of a lighted lantern over the apartment of the one with whom he had decided to stay. His son, my brother-in-law was an even greater rascal than Third Brother.

At the beginning of the revolution in 1911, we were forced to flee from Nanking, and Third Brother went to Shanghai carrying a suitcase of gold and jewelry belonging to his wife. He asked his brother-in-law to lend him a carriage, so he could take the gold to a goldsmith's shop and exchange it for money. This request was readily granted, and Third Brother set out on his errand. When they approached an open space, the driver suddenly slowed down, and a masked robber sprang from behind a wall, flung open the door of the carriage, seized the suitcase, and made off. Third Brother called the driver to his assistance, and jumped out to give chase, calling "Help! Help!" But the driver, who was paid to help the robber, did not follow. Third Brother ran until he was exhausted, and a crowd of people ran after him to help in the chase, but the thief had disappeared. A policeman arrived and questioned my brother, while the crowd listened, but nobody had seen the thief or knew where he had gone. Two children at last came forward and said they had seen a man sitting on a suitcase in front of one of the doorways in their alley. So the thief was caught, and we knew from the behavior of the driver that it was Brother-in-law who had hatched the plot in order to lay his own hands on the gold.

These are just two out of many stories I could tell, but they show that in these great households where people are without Christ, the evil that goes on is unimaginable.

As for me, I was a timid, overprotected child, hiding behind my nurse when strangers appeared, and covering my face with her apron when anyone spoke to me. Everyone who grows up in such a household is constantly hearing stories of the evil all around, and getting involved in the innumerable plots and counterplots of this ingrown society. What I saw and heard frightened me, so when I was able to discern between good and evil, and knew I was growing up, I shrank from the adult role and pondered a great deal on the vanity of life. All our family constantly sent for the Buddhist monks to chant and perform masses in the temple in our house. We had an aged Buddhist instructor, too, and he taught me to read the Buddhist classics, to say their prayers, to burn incense before their idols. I even took vegetarian vows to eat no meat, not even eggs, for twenty-five days out of each month. Buddhism, which is a religion of escape from the realities of life, only deepened my pessimism, and I applied for entrance into a Buddhist convent near us; but the Lord, who had planned my life, though I did not know it, took pity on me and prevented my taking this step.

There came a change in our family affairs. Troubles fell on us thick and fast, followed by repeated financial reverses. My father and mother had always been great lovers, and they used to talk over their family problems and come to an agreement before they acted. Of course, their greatest problem was how to provide for their huge family. My mother wanted to invest our money in some land along the Yangtse River front, just outside the city wall. "That land is cheap now and is certain to become valuable very soon as the river trade develops. Don't you see the British steamers are opening up trade here on the Yangtse? Nanking will soon become a great river port," she said.

"How can we be sure of that?" my father replied. "That water front is only a mud-walled fishing village now, with a single hulk anchored by the shore where the river steamers tie up. Surely the British will not be able to develop more trade than that. We dare not gamble on our future. There are some Europeans who have been coming to see me who have traveled all over China, and tell me there are immense beds of coal lying close to the surface of the ground in South Anhwei Province. All they need is some capital for development, and these mines will yield fabulous sums. We Chinese have destroyed all our forests by cutting down the trees for fuel. If we can sell people coal instead of wood, our family will be secure for life." Such was the line of argument, and my father prevailed. Circumstances proved later that he was wrong and she was right. He bought three coal-rich mountains and organized a mining company. The man he depended on to run the company was ignorant, and frittered the money away in

unwise expenditures. We never mined any coal. There the mountains stand to this day, and I know not who has mined them. As
for the river front, that land later proved very valuable.

Our main source of income was now lost, and other catas-
trophes followed. Just as Job was one day rich and content, and
the next day poor and sick, so my father lost one investment after
another. First came a telegram saying a big store in a distant
city had been burned; then another message telling of the loss
of another store. Next a private steamer which we owned was
sunk in the river. Had my father known the Lord, he might
have learned to say with Job, "The Lord gave, and the Lord
hath taken away; blessed be the name of the Lord." The result
was that though he still kept his official position, my father lost
his health and became so sick that we thought he would die. In
such an emergency, the Chinese custom is to make superstitious
preparations for the funeral.

I remember watching the servants clean all the hanging glass
lanterns, and open all the doors. Outside the front door appeared
a large paper sedan chair for him, paper chair-bearers, a paper
horse, and boxes of paper ghost money. Lighted incense sticks
were placed in all the incense burners, and the sweet-smelling smoke
made the air blue. In the garden, carpenters were making a huge
coffin out of fragrant wood, and in the big reception hall were
high piles of colored silk quilt covers, the children's gifts to him.
My elder sisters were busy sewing large pearls to the corners of
his hat and embroidered gowns, to serve as lights to guide his
way in the other world. We children were each given a bundle
of incense sticks, told when to light them, and when to kneel
down and cry in farewell. For at the instant he breathed his last,
all the doors must be opened for the spirit to go out, the lanterns
lit, the paper models burned, and we must light our incense sticks,
kneel down and wail in farewell. These preparations were the
sign that he was expected to die at any moment.

Suddenly, my mother appeared and called Fifth Brother and
me, saying, "You two are to go to the big Buddhist Temple and

make a vow to the idol of the City King, promising that every one of you will give your father a year from your own life if the god will prolong his life beyond the allotted span."

This temple, with all its fierce-looking idols was a terrifying place for a young girl. I remember how I shivered as we bowed to the ground before the great idol, while the tremendous bell boomed, the drums beat, and the chief monk in his yellow robes read aloud the names of the children who had vowed to give a year to our father. Coming home I decided that I must do something further to save my father's life. Chinese books are full of stories of children who have sacrificed themselves to help their parents, for filial devotion is a cardinal virtue with the Chinese. I had read in a book somewhere of a child who had saved his father's life in a heroic way, so I decided to follow his example. But to make it efficacious, I vowed that for a hundred days I would not tell anyone what I had done.

I had no idea of hygiene, so in my room I took a pair of rusty scissors, set my teeth into my forearm, pulled up the flesh and hacked off a good-sized piece. I then spread some ashes from the incense burner on the wound to stop the bleeding, tied my arm with a soiled handkerchief, and pulled my sleeve down to cover it up. Fortunately, I did not sever an artery and bleed to death. I then put the flesh in a pot and went out to the kitchen. The cook asked if he could help me, but I only shook my head. I put the flesh in water and cooked it; then took the soup to Father and begged him to drink it. As I raised his head, it fell back on my fresh wound, causing me excruciating pain. He drank the liquid and did recover, not because of the soup, but because the good Lord, whom I did not know, saw my love, heard the unspoken prayer, and healed him.

The wound got well slowly and I suffered a great deal, but I kept my arm covered so no one would know. The hundred days passed and my vow was accomplished. Later, Father and Mother found out what I had done and were deeply moved at my love for them.

CHAPTER VI

Out into the World

A MELANCHOLY UNREST filled my heart, and nowhere could I find peace. I had won my parents' affection, but it did not satisfy me. My father saw I was not happy, so he used to take me every Sunday to the theatre to see Chinese plays; but I did not like them. I often played mah-jongg all night long, and it was uncanny how I always won; but this had no fascination for me. I drank our Chinese wine which has given happy dreams to many, but it could not drive away my sadness. In our family orchestra, with my brothers and sisters, we played Chinese instruments in our garden pavilion every summer evening, but music seemed but "a clanging brass and tinkling cymbal" to me. I immersed myself in Buddhism and kept my vegetarian vows, but this only inclined me the more to pessimism. I found with the preacher in Ecclesiastes that everything was "vanity and vexation of spirit." All this outward display of wealth and pomp engendered in me something like a festering sore, for it increased my troubles rather than dispersed them.

The only solution that I could see was for me to go away from home; but I did not dare suggest this to my parents, so I poured out my heart to my nurse. "I want to attend one of those foreign missionary schools where they teach English and piano."

"But aren't you afraid they will make you 'eat Christianity'?" she asked.

"I don't want their Christianity, but I'd rather be an educated spirit than a stupid person," I reiterated again and again. She passed my confidence on to one of my brothers, and he in turn told my parents. They saw my unhappiness and arranged for me to attend a fashionable Christian girls' school in Shanghai. The registration fee was paid, the trunks were packed, and I was ready to go when my father called me to him. "I have been thinking about your leaving home and going alone to this strange city so far away. I am afraid you might get sick, so I've decided not to allow you to go." I dared not argue with him, but I was sick with disappointment. However, I did not give up hope, and the next semester I brought up the subject again. Three times I paid my registration fee, packed my trunks and prepared to go, only to be disappointed at the last moment. It was such an un-heard-of thing for a young girl to leave her home and go away to school that even though they loved me, my parents could not bring themselves to the point of carrying it out.

I still did not give up hope. I suggested to Mother as a compromise, "Let me go to this mission girls' school here in Nanking. There I will be near home and you can know what happens to me." She agreed to this, and one wonderful day I dressed up in new clothes, got into my sedan chair, and went across the city to the Leaman's home, and the Ming Deh Girls' School at Four Flagstaffs. The chair-bearers let me down at the gate, and I walked into the mission compound. There were three plain foreign-style residences and a schoolhouse, set in a lawn shaded by trees and crossed by flower-bordered walks. It all looked so neat and clean. In the Leaman's house I was impressed by the carpeted floors and clean whitewashed walls, with the sunshine streaming in through the curtains at the windows. For the first time an indescribable peace stole into my heart. A tall, thin American lady, who turned out to be Mrs. Leaman's daughter Mary, came in. She wore a grey dress with black borders, and there was something in her quiet manner and kind voice that radiated peace. Here was the inner light, serenity and strength that I had been seeking for.

"I want to register in your school so I can learn to speak English and play the piano," I said. She looked at my fashionable

The green sedan chair.

clothes and embroidered shoes and saw I was from a rich family. She asked, "What is your name? Who are your parents? Where do you live?"

"My father's name is Tsai Sung Hua. We live at Millstone Street and I am called Tsai Ling Fang."

"Mr. Tsai, the Acting-Viceroy?" she asked in astonishment. I nodded. But she looked very serious and I grew fearful as she said, "We would be very glad to have you come and learn English and piano, but we cannot take you in as a boarder. Our school is very poor, and many of the students are orphans. Our food is very coarse, and our students do the housework. I fear you would not enjoy living here since you are used to better things."

"Oh, yes! I would," I insisted. "I don't mind coarse food and poor people. I want to learn English."

"But did your mother give you permission to come to our school?"

"Oh, yes, indeed she did," I answered.

"Well, we have a rule that the parents must come here themselves and give us their permission for you to study. Can you ask your mother to come?" she asked.

"I can try," I answered. So I went home and asked my mother. She was angry at first. Why should she, a Viceroy's wife, go across the city to see those poor missionaries? But I pleaded with her and she finally consented.

The next day she got into her green sedan chair, I followed in mine, and with an escort of horsemen, we appeared at the Ming Deh Girls' School gate. There was a great commotion at the entrance, and intense excitement among the girls as we entered the house. But my mother was very gracious and Miss Leaman was very polite, so I was finally registered as a day student; Miss Leaman still insisted that they could not take the responsibility of having me live there with the poor orphans. At home my mother bought a private ricksha and hired a ricksha man just to take me across the city to school.

My first English lesson was a story about "A Deer at the Brook," and then I had an organ lesson. Some days later Miss Leaman said, "Don't you want to join our English Bible class?"

"No," I answered emphatically.

"But you can't be really educated if you don't know this Book," she explained. I didn't answer her, but in my heart I thought, "Not educated, if I don't read the Bible? What do you think about our Confucian classics? Are our Chinese scholars not educated?" However, I reluctantly agreed to join them, for though I wanted none of their Christianity, an extra English class was welcome. During the lesson period, while Miss Leaman read, "Verily, verily I say unto you," I fumed in my heart, saying to myself, "What is all this nonsense about—'Verily, verily I say unto you'? I don't understand what she is talking about."

At Christmas time I was invited to attend the service in the church, but I did not understand the meaning of Christmas. I gazed curiously at the colored paper flags strung across the church, at the bamboo trees against the walls, at the worshipers in their coarse blue cotton gowns covering their heavy padded garments. Occasionally I caught a word from the pastor, whose long sermon was incomprehensible to me. Bewildered, I turned to the students beside me. "What are they saying?" I asked one on my right. "What does that mean?" I asked the other on the left. But they were trained not to speak in church, so they only shook their heads. Then Miss Lucy Leaman came up behind me and whispered politely, "We are having worship now."

"Worship?" I thought. "I see no one to worship."

After the service, as I was stepping into my ricksha, Miss Lucy hurried down to the gate and thrust a paper parcel into my hands, and with no word of explanation she left me. I knew nothing of Christmas presents and wondered what she was giving me. I opened the parcel and found a Chinese Bible, which I disdained to read. This was my first Christmas!

The kindness of the missionaries impressed me profoundly. Every day on my way home I used to pass a ricksha coming the other way. A tall foreign lady with curly hair sat in it, and she always bowed to me and smiled. This gratuitous kindness puzzled me, too, for we Chinese are taught to speak politely to others but never think of smiling at strangers. I found out later that this was Miss Ellen Dresser, a missionary returning from her work in the southern part of the city. To this day that winning smile is one of my treasured memories, for it is the genuine evidence of God's indwelling love which never fails to convey its message of cheer.

My family saw that no harm had come to me from attending school, but because the long daily rides across the city were very tiring, they decided to send me to another school in the city of Soochow, where I could stay as a boarder. This school was especially for girls from wealthy homes, so better food and service were provided. The gates of home had opened, and I left the high walls of my childhood and passed out into the wide, wide world.

CHAPTER VII

The Light of the World

WITH THE OVERTHROW of the Manchus and the establishment of the Republic of China in 1911, western education, modern inventions and Christianity had come to China to stay. The anti-foreign riots were a thing of the past. Men's queues were forcibly cut off, and foot-binding and opium-smoking abolished by law. The Standard Oil Company of America had put kerosene lamps into people's homes. The ricksha copied from Japan was far speedier than the sedan chair. Nanking had some roads at least twenty feet wide now, and people went by horse and carriage on the longer trips to the river front. The British and American Tobacco Companies were sending their sales-men into villages and cities to sell cigarettes.

But more disturbing to the Chinese peasants than all these was a railroad opened from Shanghai to Nanking, a distance of about two hundred miles. The carriers, wheelbarrow coolies, donkey boys, boatmen and farmers saw in this railroad a threat to their living, and determined to get rid of this devilish inven-tion. Rumors spread that the god of the locomotive demanded human sacrifices. Eighth Brother was an executive for this railroad, and he suggested that we take the trip to Soochow by the new train. So Second Sister-in-law and I arrived at the Nanking Rail-road Station, and slightly awestruck, we passed the crowds of curious and angry people who were staring at the "little houses that run on wheels." The train had no sooner started from the station than a shower of bricks and stones shattered the windows. Not far out of Nanking the train came to a halt, as some peasants were lying on their faces on the tracks, determined to stop the "fire wagon" with their lives. The conductors and railroad personnel got off the train and reasoned with them for a long time before they moved. In later years, the Shanghai-Nanking Railway was said to have had the greatest number of passengers per mile of any railway in the world. The railway was a success!

Soochow is a city of beautiful homes, pagodas, winding canals, and arched bridges. It is famous for its beautiful women and scholarly men, so in the proverb it is linked with Hangchow as the other part of "Heaven below." I attended a mission girls' school there which gave advanced studies in English and music. Here I studied hard at my lessons but closed my heart to Christianity and everything connected with it. When church time came, I made excuses for staying away—I had a headache or a backache—and I threw out the medicine that they gave me. But these subterfuges did not work long, for the teachers saw through them. I was told that I must attend the services. This only increased my resistance, and I made up my mind that I was not going to "eat" their Christianity, so I used to take a Chinese novel with me to chapel and read it as I knelt at the bench. I did not like the preaching. I thought it was very unpleasant and openly opposed it. Another girl, a Miss Wu, from a high-class family similar to my own, hated this teaching too, and we used to get together and give voice to our indignation. We even started to write a book denouncing all Christian teaching, insisting that Confucius and Buddha were our teachers and that we did not want Christ.

But again God used my love for English to draw me to Himself. A famous American preacher was to speak in English in our church; for a little while I let down the bars on my heart and listened intently. His subject was "Jesus, the Light of the World," and he used an illustration that stuck in my mind. He said, "If a piece of wood is kept in a dark place, all kinds of ugly insects will hide under it. But if we expose it to the light, the insects will run away, for they love darkness and hate the light. So it is with our hearts: if we do not have Jesus, the Light of the world, in our

Bridge at Soochow

hearts, they will be dark too, and harbor all kinds of evil thoughts. The moment we receive Him and the light He brings, the evil thoughts will all be driven away."

From childhood I had especially feared all kinds of insects, so this illustration made a deep impression on me. One day while playing croquet in the yard, I saw a smooth white stone lying in the grass which reminded me of the illustration. I thrust my mallet under it and lifted it up. A big lizard, a centipede, and little bugs scurried away as the light shone in, and a voice inside me said, "You are just like this stone, smooth and white outside, and full of sin inside."

I now saw the hypocrisy of saying that I was following our Chinese traditions of love, righteousness, truth and virtue, and I knew in my heart that I was a sinner, too. I dropped my mallet and hurried to my room, recalling that Miss Mary Leaman had often spoken of the importance of prayer. I took a quick look around to be sure nobody saw me, and knelt by my bed and prayed, "Lord, forgive my sin and help me to understand Thy Word." Then I got up quickly, my heart pounding and my face all red. At last I had found peace. The burden of sin and the pessimism of unbelief had gone from my soul! I had found Christ! From that time on, I opened my heart to the study of the Bible and found comfort in it.

I told Miss Wu of my experience, and how I had found peace when I found Christ. She was impressed, and after a while, accepted Him as her Saviour, and we had happy fellowship together. We did not tell our families, nor did we join the church at that time. Yet life was changed for us both: the old unrest was gone and all the world was a beautiful garden of the Lord to us. In my old home, Father used to have tiny fragrant jasmine flowers wired into pretty shapes for us girls to wear in our hair. I thought it was foolishness then, for I never saw any beauty in them. It had been the same way with music and poetry. Now there was a fountain of love in my heart and every bird, flower and blade of grass, every cloud and every star, sang a hymn of praise to God its Creator, and my heart sang with them.

Miss Wu was engaged to a young man whose sister was one of the students at our school. She wrote home that his fiancée was "eating Christianity." The Wu family soon heard this, and both families were furious. One day she was called from the classroom to find a relative waiting for her in the guest room. "Your parents sent me to take you home. Pack your things and be prepared to leave immediately. I have a houseboat waiting to take us up the canal," he said.

On the boat, he brought her a knife and a rope, saying, "You have disgraced your family by eating this Christian religion. Didn't we warn you not to listen to it? Your family are very angry and do not want you as their daughter any more. If you do not promise to give up your Christianity now and return to our religion, you will have to choose between this rope to hang yourself, this knife to stab yourself, or the canal to drown yourself."

With a white face she answered, "I cannot give up Jesus. He died for my sins to open for me the way to Heaven. I belong to Him. You may take my life, but you cannot harm my soul." The relative was awed by her quiet determination, and did not force her to commit suicide. At home neither the angry accusations nor cruel punishment of the family could shake her, so finally they gave up the attempt. I saw her many times in later years and know she remained true to Christ, but the whole family have always opposed Christianity.

The Buddhists teach that the living children may help the deceased parent in the other world; my father had died, and my third sister wanted to send a gift to his spirit. She ordered a paper model made on a life-size scale, of our home at Nanking, completely furnished, even with servants, shoes and chopsticks. It is the superstitious belief that when this paper house is burned, it goes to the spirit world for the deceased to live in. To her it was an impressive display of filial affection; to the Buddhists monks it was a handsome source of income; to me as I see it now, it was a colossal exhibition of folly.

Each part was constructed in advance and assembled on the date named in a large, open place. She had already sent invitations to many friends and hired many Buddhist monks to say masses for the dead. Then she prevailed on me, as the only unmarried daughter in Soochow, who bore the name of Tsai, to be family representative and accompany the monks. I was just a young Christian at the time, and still wanted to honor my father; nevertheless, my conscience made me acutely unhappy all during the proceedings and for a long time after.

When the day came, I followed the chief monk, and a long line of monks followed me on a tour of this paper mansion. The chief monk first entered one chamber and while he chanted a long mass dedicating the room to my father's spirit, I knelt prostrate on the floor, the other monks around us, some beating drums, some clanging cymbals, some burning incense, and all chanting together. This procedure was repeated in each room and the whole ceremony took a day. At the end they made a great circle around the house, and chanted the masses again. I then handed a paper key to the head monk, who hung it on the door and set fire to the paper palace, while I remained prostrate on the ground till the last ember had turned to black ashes. After this, all the guests were invited to a feast.

You can imagine how my heart was torn by conflict: on the one hand trying to justify myself for doing my duty to Father and Sister, and on the other, unable to still the voice inside which said, "You're a Christian now, and should have no part with Buddhist monks. You have accepted Christ for your Lord—how can you still pray to Buddha?" The cloud of that spiritual defeat hung over me for a long time, until I learned that when "we confess our sins, Jesus is faithful and just to forgive us our sins, and to cleanse us from all unrighteousness." This experience also taught me never to compromise with heathenism.

Not long after this, I was baptized and joined the church, though I still lacked courage to tell my mother. But vacation time was drawing near when I had to go home, and I knew it would be better to tell them in advance. So, as the easier course, I wrote my sister-in-law and asked her to tell my mother what I had done. I soon had an angry letter from Mother telling me to come home immediately.

I remember entering the parlor of our home and seeing Mother chatting with my brothers; when she saw me she burst into tears. Sixth Brother's face flushed with anger. He said bitterly, "You have disgraced the whole family! We meant you to get an education, not to eat this foreign religion!" Then, seeing a Bible and hymnbook in my hand, he snatched them away, tore them up and threw the pieces in my face. I was shocked at this savage behavior from a member of my own family, for we had always been polite to one another; but I said nothing and silently looked to God. Suddenly I saw a vision of Christ on the cross, a crown of thorns on His head and with nails in His hands, and I knew He had suffered for my sins; had purchased my head with His crown, and my hands with His nails. Was there anything I couldn't bear for Him who had suffered so much for me? But to them I still said nothing.

Now they began talking together and sensibly decided that since there was nothing they could do to take this faith from my heart, they could only keep me at home as a kind of prisoner; but they found many ways of mocking me. When I bowed my head to say grace at the table, someone would remark, "If you have a headache you had better leave the table." At other times they commanded me to leave the table, saying, "If you do that, the devils will come out!" If one of my sisters found me praying beside my bed, she said, "She is sick. We must call the doctor." And when the time came to worship the ancestors, they dragged me along and threatened, "If you don't worship your ancestors, they will punish us." As I walked through the house, the servants stared at me and whispered together. Even the children were sternly charged to keep away from me. But I did not argue; I only prayed for wisdom, and God gave me grace.

One day, Eighth Brother, who was then more friendly than

the others, approached me with a proposition. He had read Dickens' *Tale of Two Cities* and liked the story. "Let's translate this book into Chinese together," he said. I was glad of the opportunity to talk to him as we worked over the translation. One day he said, "Tell me about Christianity and why you became a Christian." I told him about the stone with the insects underneath, and my conviction of sin; the prayer to God and the new peace and joy I had found. "That was a remarkable experience," he replied. "I have noticed that in spite of the way we treat you now, you seem much happier than you used to be. I think I would like to believe, too."

He even told Mother he was interested in Christianity, whereupon she burst into tears again and cried, "I can't bear it! I can't bear it! It is bad enough to have my daughter believing this religion. I will give her to anyone, send her to any kind of home to have her soon married and keep our name from disgrace! But you are my son! I depend on you to offer food and burn incense to me when I die. I forbid you to speak to her." After this she cried seven days and seven nights.

One day she called me to her, saying, "Seventh Daughter, I want to betroth you. Here, let me show you the beautiful clothes and fine jewels I have set aside for your trousseau."

But as I gazed at the finery, I said, "Oh, Mother, Jesus is more to me than anything on earth! I cannot do this!"

She thought of another expedient and some days later spoke to me again, saying, "Seventh Daughter, I won't have you here in this house deluding your brothers with your Christian religion. You must return to Soochow and finish your schooling there." My family saw the futility of keeping me a prisoner at home, and to my great joy sent me back to Soochow.

CHAPTER VIII

The Fruit of the Spirit

I WAS ONE of the first Chinese girls to graduate from a high school in China, an event so rare at that time that I was offered many positions. The principal of my school asked me to be vice-principal; another missionary asked me to be General Secretary of the Y.W.C.A.; and the mayor of Soochow asked me to tour the cities of the province and promote women's education. But I had an ambition dearer than these: to return home and lead my family to the Saviour, and have them enter into the same peace and joy that had driven away my dark pessimism. Various friends urged against this, saying I should work for all China and not stay in one place. But I felt clearly that I should go to Nanking, and refused the other offers. In Nanking I went to call on Miss Mary Leaman. "Would you like to have me help you in the evangelistic work?" I asked. She looked at me in astonishment, because such a thought had never occurred to her; but she was pleased and acccepted my offer, agreeing that I was to live at home and do my work from there.

My mother was the head of the family now. If she accepted Jesus, others would follow. I approached her but she would not listen to me, and coldly repelled all advances. Again and again I urged her, but she only said, "When I am dead and in my coffin, with the lid fastened down, then and then only will I believe in your Jesus."

Her love of music, however, was the entering wedge for Christ. One day when she heard me sing "He leadeth me," she remarked, "That's a pretty tune! Sing it over again to me." So I sang it again and then taught it to her, making no explanations.

Her love of stories was another. Since she could not read, she often would say, "Tell me a story." So I told her stories from the Bible without saying they were Christian, and she loved them.

Her opium-smoking habit proved the final wedge that opened the door to her heart. After Nanking had fallen to the revolutionaries and the Manchu Dynasty had been overthrown, the Republic of China was established; a new law was passed abolishing opium-smoking and imposing punishment on opium-users. Mother feared breaking the law and tried to stop the habit herself; but it was impossible. I told her of a Christian hospital for women in Nanking where doctors would help her, and finally persuaded her to go.

Breaking the opium habit was an agonizing experience, lasting for many weeks. When Miss Leaman brought her flowers and food that she could eat, she was grateful; and she appreciated the fact that we prayed for her every evening. One day she told me, "If your Jesus will take away this appetite, I will believe Him."

"Don't say 'If Jesus will take it away,' just believe that He will," I said.

That night she had a vision of Jesus standing before her and covering her with the light of His glory. That was the secret of victory for Mother; gradually she was relieved of the craving, and could take food freely.

She was a new woman the day she went home, bubbling over with joy. She showed her new allegiance in a forth-right break with the past. She went to the family temple and addressed the idols, saying, "You have deceived me all these years, but I am not going to be deceived by you any longer." Then she picked up the idols one by one and threw them on the ground, stamping on them until they were in bits; but there was one idol she set aside—a gilded goddess of Mercy which originally had a pearl headdress and lungs and a gold heart. This idol had been worshiped by members of our family for over one hundred years. Later when Miss Leaman came to visit us, my mother gave the idol to her. "This is a keepsake for you. You have helped me to turn from idols and believe in Jesus. You shall have it to show that the Tsai family idols have all been destroyed."

When Eighth Brother heard of mother's conversion and deliverance from the opium habit, he and his wife came home from Shanghai where he was working, to make their confession of Christ. Then in the little chapel on Dye Factory Street, which Mr. Leaman had built, Mother, Eighth Brother and his wife, Second Brother and his wife, and two cousins were baptized together.

After this Mother and I became inseparable companions and fellow-workers. She started a family prayer group and invited her neighbors to attend. Such condescension was unheard of, and the neighbors came willingly, eager to see our house. I remember a Mrs. Lu who attended regularly. She and her husband, happily married for many years, kept a little variety shop. One day she came to us in tears. Her husband had brought a second wife into their home. To Mrs. Lu this was intolerable, and she wanted to kill herself.

Mother said, "Why don't you ask Jesus to help you?"

"How could Jesus help me?" she asked in astonishment.

"Ask Jesus to make the 'Little Wife' leave your husband. Come, we will pray about it together."

It was not long before Mrs. Lu came to the evening service again, her face beaming with joy and her heart bursting with good news. "What do you think has happened? The 'Little Wife' ran away yesterday, taking all my husband's money and clothes! He is furious and swore he would never see her again; but I know it was Jesus who answered our prayer."

After this Mr. Lu began to come to our church, became an earnest Christian and was later made a deacon.

Mother was about sixty at this time, and it grieved her that she could not read the Bible; so she called her little grandson

Ever-cheer to her and told him to bring his picture books and teach her to recognize Chinese characters. So the old lady and the child teacher studied together until she was able to read the New Testament.

Mother now enjoyed entertaining missionaries. Miss Leaman was the first one to be invited to our home, and I remember the day she arrived. She stepped out of her sedan chair, carrying an unusually large hen, which she presented to Mother. Mother was delighted with the hen for it laid a double-yolked egg every day! Another guest she enjoyed was Miss Ruth Paxson, who spoke her own Peking dialect and had fasted and prayed that she might be given power to break the opium habit. Among many other guests were Miss Alice Longdon, my loving piano teacher, who later married the Rev. Wesley Smith, and Miss Mary Culler White, my faithful friend, the humble but indefatigable evangelist who did a far-reaching work for the Chinese women in the area around Soochow. They were both a great help to me during my school days. Miss Mabel Lee often came with her guitar, and we sang hymns together. She called our home "The Church in the House." My brothers and the servants were especially glad when Mr. Drummond came, for he helped them with their spiritual problems. One of the early missionaries who came soon after Mr. Leaman, he stayed in Nanking through all the riots, wars and political turnovers that had been our lot from the beginning of missionary work in Nanking.

My mother's gifts that in years gone by had been given to Buddhist temples, were now sent to those who served the Lord. One year the money that was to have been spent for her birthday was divided between the Mueller Orphan Homes in England, and the Jewish Mission work of Ruth Angel, in New York.

After mother's conversion, I was away from home much of the time, speaking and interpreting at various meetings and conferences. The Holy Spirit was working in our home, not only among the family, but among the servants as well. One of the maids washing the clothes was suddenly convicted that her heart needed cleansing. She ran to Mother and knelt down, crying, "Lord Jesus, please wash my heart of all sin." A slave girl named Double-Joy had been indifferent to all appeals; but when an earthquake set the windows rattling, she fell on her face in terror, crying, "Jesus, save me!" My youngest sister's husband was a judge who had mocked us for believing; but one day, to Mother's complete surprise, he came and said to her, "I want to go to Tenghsien Theological Seminary and study to be a minister. Would Seventh Sister make arrangements for me to enter?" I did, and he went there to study.

One summer evening, I had just returned from a conference up north, and was sitting with the family eating a vegetable stew. They told me that one of our cousins had suddenly gone crazy. She had taken a bucket of water to our Ancestral Hall and started washing the tablets of our ancestors—to our non-Christian relatives' way of thinking, a terrible insult. For two weeks she had refused to eat anything they gave her, but went to the gutter and ate the worms she found there, so her brother had chained her in one of the rooms. Just at that moment there was a rattle of chains in the courtyard, and my family jumped up and ran out of the room. I gazed at my cousin's horrible, grimacing face, now thin and sallow, with long hair hanging about her shoulders. It was a hot summer night, but she wore a padded jacket and padded shoes.

"Seventh Sister's Jesus, save me!" she cried again and again. I had to think quickly, so I said, "If you ask Jesus, He will save you, but you must do what you are told. Sit down!" She sat down obediently enough, and I dished out a bowlful of stew and gave it to her. "Eat this," I said. She took it without a word and ate it. Then I gave her another bowlful, and she ate that, too. The rest of the family had returned by this time and were standing around looking at her. "In the name of Jesus, I command this evil spirit to leave you," I said. Immediately she slumped forward, her head drooping on the table. All the demon power which had enabled her to break the chain, was gone. We carried her to her room, and she was completely well from that day. Later she went to Miss Dresser's Bible school to study.

Sometime after this cousin had been cured, her brother was brought home from school, dying of typhoid fever. I, too, was down with a fever. As I lay on my bed reading the words of Jesus to the dying thief, "This day thou shalt be with me in Paradise," I seemed to hear a voice saying: "Why don't you go and speak to your cousin? This may be his last chance." I thought of many excuses for not going, but could not drive his image from my thoughts. Finally I got up and went over to his apartment. He was very ill indeed, but recognized me. "Cousin," I said, "don't you want to accept the Lord Jesus?" A smile lit up his face and he gasped, "That is just what I was thinking of. Won't you send for the minister and have me baptized?"

The minister came and baptized him, and was surprised that my cousin could answer all the questions. I now called Double-Joy, the slave girl, and told her to take care of the young master. While she was nursing him, he opened his eyes, exclaiming, "I see it! I see it! How beautiful it is! But the gate is shut, I can't go in! Oh, why is the gate shut? I want to go in!"

"Be patient," said Double-Joy, wisely. "Maybe the time has not come to open the gate."

"That's right," he replied; "I do have something more to do. Send for my family. I want to speak to them." So his brother and sister-in-law came in and stood beside him, while he fixed his eyes on them, saying, "I plead with you to accept Christ. Just a while ago, I saw the heavenly halls. They were so beautiful and I wanted to go in, but the gates were shut. Now I see them again and the gates are open at last." And with radiant face, he entered through those gates.

Such a testimony would have moved most people; but the Word tells us of times when seed falls on stony ground. To this day, so far as I know, the brother and sister-in-law are still hardened in their hearts to the call of Christ. But Double-Joy married a Christian man and they went to their village to live for Christ.

CHAPTER IX

Seed Sown in Good Ground

*E*VERY SUMMER we invited students from seven of the girl's schools to spend their vacation with us. Part of my work was teaching in a government normal school for girls, and I had about two hundred students in my classes. I used to talk to them in the intermissions about Christianity. Seventy-two of them accepted Jesus, and they came frequently to my home and to Bible classes in our church. One day two sisters, Spring-Hill and May-Hill, came to me sobbing, "Oh, Miss Seven, did you read the article in the newspaper reviling you?"

"No," I replied; "what did it say?"

"It said, 'The Government normal school has employed a music teacher and gotten a Christian evangelist instead, who is teaching all the girls to cry, "God! God!" and making Christians of them. The parents are up in arms!'"

"Never mind," I said. "To be reviled for the Lord's sake is a great honor."

Three cousins named Long, from the normal school, came to our home frequently. They loved to sing "Heaven Is My Home." One afternoon three strange women appeared at our gate demanding to see me. They rushed into my sitting room without waiting to be announced. Each one took out a ball of opium about the size of a small nut and said, "We are the mothers of the three Long cousins. They are all we have in the world, and we sent them to school so they would be able to take care of us when we are old. You are teaching them to sing about 'Heaven! Heaven!' all day long. When we die there will be nobody to send money and

70

food to our spirits in the next world. Now unless you promise to keep them away from here, we will each swallow this opium and die in your house."

This was the worst threat a Chinese could make to his enemy. I tried to reason with them. "Suppose I kept a shoe shop. It would be right to try to sell shoes to anyone who came to my shop, wouldn't it? But if I went out on the street and dragged people in and made them buy my shoes, it would not be right, would it? Now you are the girls' mothers. It is *your* responsibility to forbid them to come here! But if they come of their own free will, it is my right and duty as a Christian to try to persuade them to become Christians, for that was Christ's commission to us."

"We have forbidden them to come, but they disobey us! Just now we had to lock them up in order to come here ourselves. No, you must forbid them coming here."

"I can't do that," I said.

"Well, if you don't, we'll just stay here with you."

"You are welcome to stay with me as long as you wish, if you don't mind our poor tea and tasteless rice," I replied. But they kept on arguing with me and would not leave till two in the morning.

The next day the three girls came to see me, and smilingly asked, "Do you know what our mothers said when they came home?"

"No, tell me."

"Well, they said, 'Fortunately for us, we three went together to see that Miss Tsai, and had one another for support and help. If one of us had gone alone, she would certainly have persuaded her to become a Christian.'"

Just at the time the article against me appeared in the newspaper, the normal school invited a Miss Plum, from Tientsin, to be their dean. She was small and pretty, energetic and discerning, but she was an atheist. While she was at home writing her letter of acceptance, her uncle came in to her study. He held a copy of the newspaper, and, pointing to the article about me, said, "Read

The three cousins in the Tsai garden

this! You'd better not go to Nanking. I fear you too may be inveigled into believing Christianity."

Miss Plum read the article; slamming her hand on the table, she exclaimed, "Don't worry, Uncle! The whole world may turn to Christianity" (and here she smote her breast) "but I will never believe."

As soon as she reached Nanking, she started to make it hard for those at the school who were Christians. Spring-Hill and her friend Joy-Bell, burst in on me one day with news. "A devil has come to our school! You know those leather-bound New Testaments you gave us students? Well, we heard Miss Plum was anti-Christian, so we hid them under our mattresses. She heard about them and searched our dormitories, seizing thirty-seven of them. Then she ordered a heap of straw piled in the yard and called us all to stand there before it. As the fire was lit she tore the Testaments and threw them into the leaping flames. Then she sternly told us, 'If any student is caught going to Miss Tsai's house again, she will be expelled.' Oh, Miss Seven! this woman will be either a devil indeed or a general for the Lord. We must pray for her, because we admire her ability, but we fear her power and want her to be saved." Those two students were very loving in trying to win her for the Lord.

When I went to the school I met Miss Plum in the hall and stopped to speak to her. She hardened her face, turned her eyes away, and passed me by. The students in my domestic science class were giving an afternoon tea, and I asked the student assistant to invite Miss Plum and place me next to her at the table. When I sat down beside her, Miss Plum's face flushed with anger, for she saw through the plan. She turned away and would not speak to me. It looked as if we were up against a stone wall, but we put her name on our prayer list and prayed for her faithfully.

The missionaries at Four Flagstaffs were also interested in these normal school girls and invited them to a Christmas program at Ming Deh School. Miss Plum accompanied them as their chaperon, so this gave Miss Leaman a chance to meet her, and invite her to a dinner; but Miss Plum coldly refused all invitations. But prayers continued without ceasing. One day when the girls were having a prayer meeting at Miss Leaman's house and singing "For You I Am Praying," who should be announced but Miss Plum herself? She was very gracious and joined in the service, while they read the whole of Philippians together. Though she was still very reserved, some seed was undoubtedly sown that day and it began to take root in her heart.

Soon after this, there was a plague epidemic in Nanking and all schools were closed. It was Miss Plum's duty to accompany some of the students on a houseboat trip up the canal to their homes. As the boat was poled slowly out into the country, along green banks and fresh fields of wheat, the beauty of nature gripped her heart and a voice inside her said clearly, "Who made all this beauty? You are an atheist, but can you explain how all this came about? You know there could not be a wonderful world like this without a Creator!"

"A Creator," Miss Plum thought. "That is what the Christians say. Perhaps there is a God after all—I would like to read that book—Philippians, again. Just reading the Bible won't make me a Christian." So she began to read the Bible secretly, and her keen mind was no longer able to gainsay her hungry heart. One day she called on me in my home, saying in her direct way, "Do you have to keep the Lord's Day if you are a Christian?" I answered her in Jesus' words, "He that putteth his hand to the plough and looketh back is not fit for the kingdom of God." Her face fell and she turned abruptly away. Later she told me, "Your answer was like a bucket of cold water poured down my back, for it was my duty in the school to work on the Lord's Day."

I was called away to a conference at Peitaiho. One day while there, I had a letter from Joy-Bell which said, "Miss Plum has resigned from the normal school to become a Christian."

After this, the principal of Ming Deh School immediately invited her to be their dean, and Miss Plum, Joy-Bell and Spring-Hill worked with us for several happy years. Later they joined an indigenous group of Chinese Christians who have no paid workers, and who teach that it is the duty of every Christian to do his own missionary work. These three faithful women have been in charge of all their literary production and have served on the inner council. This group has had an extraordinary growth in the past years. It has spread over China and the islands of the Pacific.

We planned a crusade to reach all classes of people in the city. We visited Chinese government schools and invited the principals and teachers to attend a Bible class in one of our homes, and we invited the students to a class at our chapel on Dye Factory Street. We also enrolled in a half-day school one hundred and fifty girls who had never had a chance to go to school when they were young. How this school started is an interesting story of a small seed that grew into a great tree.

Miss Emma Strode, a friend in West Chester, Pennsylvania, had sent us a gift of two big dolls that could shut their eyes and say "Mama," and the fame of these dolls spread like wildfire through our neighborhood. Children, girls, and people of all ages came to see them. One girl who had seen them the day before brought some friends and shyly asked, "Will you please show my friends the talking dolls? They want to see if they are real babies." When I brought them out they stretched eager hands to hold the dolls.

"What beautiful clothes! But they aren't like our Chinese clothes."

"Look at the eyes! They open and shut."

"Look at the hair! It's real."

"Listen to the baby cry! Is it a real American baby?"

Soon another group appeared, and then another, till there seemed no end to the crowds asking to see the wonder dolls. While we were amused at the great stir caused by the dolls, we pondered how to turn their interest to more constructive ends. Suddenly the idea came: "Let's open a half-day school for these older girls who have never been to school. They can work at home in the mornings and study here in the afternoons."

This school met a great need; our chapel was soon filled with rows of smiling girls holding bundles of books tied up in colored handkerchiefs. We called it the "Gen Seng [Born Again] Half-Day School." The girls earnestly applied themselves to reading the Bible and reciting it page after page.

We invited the adults to church by advertizing "Fishing Meetings." The girls were eager to bring their parents and relatives to these special services. Later the names of many of these parents and relatives appeared on the list of our church members. In a few years other churches followed, and many half-day schools were organized in Nanking and elsewhere. Some girls who had learned to read went on to higher schools, and some of them became evangelists. So the two "Mama Dolls" did a good missionary work, and who can tell how far their influence has gone?

I loved to do hospital visitation, and I found it was a good thing to take flowers, fruit, puffed rice, a comb, and postcards and pencils along; for I saw that many of the patients closed their eyes and turned their faces away when we approached, to show that they did not want us to talk to them about Christianity. If I saw a feverish patient, I'd say, "Would you like me to comb back your hair for you?" and the eyes would open in surprise and appreciation. The gifts removed the barriers. Sometimes I'd spot a country woman and ask if she wanted to send a letter to her family. Invaribly she would be delighted. I sat by her side and wrote while she dictated, and then I read it over for her approval. The following week, perhaps, I often had the opportunity to read the answer she had received. In these ways, people were won for Christ.

Mrs. William Stewart, sister of Dr. W. W. White, founder of Biblical Seminary, New York, opened her home for a Bible class for wives of important government officials. Among the women who came was the wife of the governor. She was a northerner dressed in outlandish clothes, with an elaborate, but ugly, hairdress; among the other women she looked like an ugly duckling. She invited me to visit her home, And when I arrived, she called her servant to me and said, "Tell my amah how to dress my hair properly." When this was accomplished, she said, "Will you please lend me some of your clothes for my tailor to copy? I like the clothes you wear." When I agreed to this, her next request was, "I can't read, and have no education, but will you teach me to knit? And, oh, I want to learn to play the piano, too!" She was so eager to look and act right that I helped her all I could, and she was very proud of her accomplishments. I was pleased with my "ugly duckling" who had turned into "a swan." One day she invited twelve missionaries to a feast in her home. When the feast was over, she announced, "Now I am going to play the piano for you." She sat down and played "Jesus Loves Me" through three times, and turned around to face her guests, saying, "Jesus loves me, now I am going to love Jesus."

One Sunday afternoon before our women's service, an old lady of eighty years, Mrs. Summer, beckoned to me to sit down beside her. "I want to tell you something," she said. "You know my family have all gone to the West and left me alone to care for the house. I have very little to live on, but God has taken care of me. One day last year, I saw a nice green plant growing in one of my empty courtyards. I looked at it. It was like *joo-hua-lao,* my favorite vegetable, but I was not sure until I asked a neighbor, who recognized it. 'Where did it come from?' I asked myself. 'I didn't plant it and there never has been any here before. A bird must have dropped the seed here, so it grew in between the stones. I think God sent the bird to help me.' So I watered it and took away the stones, and cultivated the ground. It grew fast and spread. After a while I plucked off a small basketful of leaves and took them to a neighbor to see.

" 'Where did you get those nice *joo-hau-lao* leaves?' she asked.

" 'God planted the seed in my garden and I watered it,' I said.

" 'I'll give you twenty cents for them,' was her answer.

"I was very happy to get the money and went back to cultivate my plants again. They grew and spread till they filled the court-

Moon gates in Tsai home

yard. I had to work hard watering and hoeing every evening all summer. I have been able to sell all I grow, and how much money do you think I made this year?"

"I couldn't guess," I answered.

"Twenty dollars! Think of that! Now the Lord has given to me, and I am going to give a tenth back to Him." She pulled out two dollars, as her contribution for the church work.

"So the seed fell on good ground, and did yield fruit that sprang up and increased; and brought forth, some thirty, and some sixty, and some a hundred."

CHAPTER X

My Watchtower

I N MY HOME at Millstone Street, I had my own apartment with a bedroom and study opening to a high-walled garden. A winding incline led up to a glassed-in tower in a corner of the courtyard; there I could sit and look down on the treetops of my garden, and on the flowers and trees in the bigger garden on the other side. I also looked down on the grey-tiled roofs of the houses beyond, stretching as far as the city wall. Even in winter, there were blossoms; a yellow flowered plum tree bloomed even when there was snow, and filled the air with rich fragrance. We call it the Twelfth Month Plum, and we had many of these trees in our garden. During the warm weather, birds love our gardens. Our Chinese robin, black-coated and yellow-billed, was my steady songster. Sometimes in the beginning of summer, I'd awaken to a liquid musical call and look out to see a flash of bright yellow. Then I knew that the oriole had come to spend his vacation with me. At nights during the harvest season, I'd hear the Indian cuckoo flying overhead and warning the farmers, "The wheat is ripe, plant the rice." This tower, with its green panorama, became my prayer room, and here I spent many happy hours.

One morning while I was writing in my study, the maid brought me some letters. Among them was one from America. The envelope, the handwriting and the postmark had become increasingly precious, for this correspondence started five years before while I was still in school at Soochow. I remember the day when I had been called into the office of Miss Martha Pyle, our principal. This American woman was my ideal teacher, and I was always thrilled to have her send for me. On this occasion my pastor was sitting there, too. Both smiled and motioned to me to sit down. The pastor laid a letter in my hand and asked me to read it. It was a proposal of marriage from a young professor in the men's university. I had seen him and knew who he was. Each time after appearing in public at a music recital I would receive many such letters, but had never answered one of them. I blushed as I read this letter and handed it back without a word. I did not know what to say.

"Miss Tsai," my pastor said, "your principal and I have consulted together and we feel this is an exceptional young man. He is an outstanding teacher and a Christian gentleman. We urge you to consider this proposal seriously."

"Yes, indeed, Christiana," my principal added. "I know the young man is the only Christian in his family, and he is considered the finest young man they have on the faculty. His principal has also sent me a letter asking me to be middleman for him. I don't know when such a request has given me greater pleasure, for I have such high regard for both of you, and feel this would be an ideal marriage. Please do consider it."

I had every reason to respect the young man, but since I was embarrassed I did not answer them, nor did I answer his letter. However, the young man was persistent in writing, and others got to know about it. Some of the teachers tried to persuade me, but I still paid no attention. When I returned to Nanking, he continued to send me so many letters that Brother, who handled most of the mail, soon came to recognize the handwriting and was curious.

"Who is this friend who sends you so many letters?" he asked one day while we were at dinner. Though I tried to appear unconcerned, I blushed. "Oh, ho! She blushes! I must look into this. It is a man's handwriting."

Mother now broke in. "You never told me about this person. Have you been answering his letters? Who is the man?"

I was in a corner and had to tell them of the young professor's proposal. "That sounds like a good young man. Twenty-one years old, did you say? I don't see how you could make a happier marriage. Why don't you answer him?" she asked.

"She's too embarrassed to write," Brother said, "so I will write for her." And so began a correspondence that changed my respect into admiration, and my admiration into love, and the university professor into my hero. We agreed that he should go to America to get his doctor's degree before we were married. So he went to America while I remained at home. In his last year at the American university, the spirit of his letters began to change. He had been an out-and-out Christian, but now the books he read made him skeptical. He wrote: "All these stories in the Bible about the virgin birth of Jesus, and the miracles He was supposed to have performed, could not possibly be true. They are no better than the Greek myths." Another time he scoffed at the Bible Institute students, saying, "They think they have only to take a tract in hand, and sit in a rocking chair, and, presto, they are saved." I was studying a Bible correspondence course at this time, and these remarks gave me deep pain. I wrote again and again, trying to show him that every page in the Bible is inspired by the Holy Spirit, and that "The secret things belong unto the Lord our God: but those things which are revealed belong unto us and to our children forever, that we may do all the words of this law." (Deut. 29:29). But my letters did not avail to change his mind, and I was unable to change my faith. Mother, who was pleased about the marriage, was now enthusiastically getting my trousseau ready. I could not tell her my grief which I kept locked in my heart.

Evening after evening, I paced up and down my garden, or knelt in the watchtower, praying for him and talking to my Lord. "He is a Christian. He has confessed that he is a child of God, and yet he does not believe in the deity of my Lord. How can we

My watchtower

ever be happy if we cannot have fellowship in our faith? What shall I do? What *shall* I do?"

Then one day I looked at this letter with mixed feelings of longing, hope and pain. Could it be that he had changed his mind about God's Word at last? But as I opened the letter and read it, my heart turned to stone. He told me of his graduation, of his doctor's degree, and how eager he was to come back to China and to me. But there was no mention of any change of mind concerning the things that mattered to me.

I took the letter in my hand and went up to the watchtower, but my feet were as heavy as lead. I spread the letter before the Lord, and a great battle began then and there. Should I follow my hero and deny my Lord, or should I follow my Lord and deny my hero? But I could not give up one or the other, and I went down with the battle still undecided. Day after day, night after night, the struggle went on.

> Should I follow my hero and deny my Lord, or
> Should I follow my Lord and deny my hero?
> My Lord or my hero?
> My hero or my Lord?

Then something happened. One day in the tower my eyes fell on a picture of Christ in Gethsemane, and I was transported in spirit. I understood His agony and He understood mine, so then and there I yielded myself and He satisfied me completely. Going down I was able to sing, but when I was seated at the typewriter, my fingers refused to move. How could I write that letter and break off the five years of happy fellowship, the many happy dreams we had shared together? But it had to be done, and I was given the strength to do it. I have never regretted the step. Since that day my Saviour's love has never failed me, and our fellowship has grown sweeter as the years have gone by.

CHAPTER XI

Out into the Highway

$\mathcal{S}$ OME APPARENTLY trivial incident often serves as the pivot upon which a man's destiny may turn; what seems mere chance may determine another's fatal choice; and a word spoken in jest may rouse the urge in someone which will work itself out in a lifetime career. But the Christian who looks back on his beginnings, finds that there was nothing accidental. There were no unfortunate incidents that marred his destiny; God, according to the good counsel of His will, had planned all his life, circumstance by circumstance, to prepare him for the work He intended him to do.

The incident which aroused my urge to learn English was trivial and amusing. While I was still a little girl, my older brothers were learning English. As boys will, they showed off their ability, and I, as a little sister, naturally wanted to learn. But try as I might, I could not pronounce the first words they tried to teach me, "breakfast, dinner and supper"; so they laughed at me. "Run away, little sister, you're hopeless! Your tongue is too blunt. You need a pointed tongue to speak English."

This stirred in me a wild ambition to excel them in English. This same urge led me to Ming Deh girls' school and my first contact with Christianity, and later to listen to a preacher's sermon on the memorable day led to my conversion. Now this love of English was to lead me all over China in the years 1914 to 1920.

An American millionaire, Milton Stewart, who was also a humble Christian, in one day distributed three million dollars for

Islands off the South China coast

evangelistic work, and much of that money was used in China. Prominent Christian leaders from America were invited to hold meetings in many centers in China. In these evangelistic meetings I had the rare privilege of interpreting for Miss Ruth Paxson, Dr. Griffith Thomas, Dr. Charles Trumbull, and others. Since they spoke mostly to the Christians, I often had special services for the non-Christians as well. We spoke to Chinese Christian leaders at the seaside conference in Peitaiho in the north, and at Kuling in the mountains of Central China. We also spoke to teachers and students of Chinese government schools, and the Christian missionary colleges and high schools in many of the large cities; to nurses in hospitals, and most of all, to the crowds in churches of various denominations. When there was no building large enough to hold the people, tents were erected. Milton Stewart did an inestimable amount of good for the world on that day when he gave a fortune for evangelistic work. The money gave pre-eminence to the gospel message, it helped link up scattered missionary effort, it trained the Christian Chinese leaders, it put good Christian literature in the hands of hundreds of thousands of people, and it scattered the Word far and wide.

China was enjoying a period of comparative peace while the rest of the world was at war. We could travel freely from one place to another, for many of the large centers were linked by modern transportation. We went from Nanking to Peking, and from Peking to Hankow, in the west, by railway. We traveled by river steamers, entering the Yangtse from the world port of Shanghai. We sailed up its broad yellow waters, past low, marshy banks, overtaking many picturesque sailboats along the way, till we caught the first glimpse of blue hills. These lines of hills extending to the horizon, steadily increased in height as we sailed west. We stopped at the treaty ports of Chinkiang, Nanking, Wuhu, Anking, Kiukiang and Hankow. At Hankow we changed to the powerful steamers that took us through the rapids of the spectacular Yangtse Gorges, into West China. Another time we took a coast steamer from Tientsin, in the north, and stopped at the beautiful Chefoo and Tsingtao ports, before coming back to Shanghai. At other times we went by coast steamers winding among the countless rocky islands that dot the South China coast, sometimes passing the yellow waters of a river-mouth, where sails of a fleet of fishing boats punctuated the water like exclamation points. Farther south the mountains became more rugged, the water a pure green, the style of junks changed, and we entered the lovely ports of Foochow, Amoy, Swatow and Hongkong.

In this way I had the opportunity of visiting eleven out of the eighteen provinces of China, and seeing the centers of Christian missions, and the wide scope of Christian activity. This was a transition era: the day of the pioneer missionary was passing and the Chinese church was growing up and beginning to call its own pastors and leaders. The children of the first generation Christian families were educated and ready for leadership, and the schools were pouring out an increasing stream of students. Who can estimate the results of missionary service in China? It made Christ known; it built churches, schools, orphanages and hospitals far and wide; it opened the door for women to enter the schools and have the same opportunities as men; it helped rouse the people to the evils of foot-binding for women, and opium-smoking; it healed the sick and brought comfort to the blind, the deaf, the dumb and the lepers; it brought knowledge of sanitation, fed famine victims, and cared for the war sufferers; it helped prepare Chinese of the following generation to take over the missionaries' work, to carry on their own evangelistic campaigns, and build their own churches; it showed the infinite value of a human soul in God's eyes, and wherever the light of the gospel shone, it enlightened that society so that it soon outstripped other places in its progress toward modern culture.

As for me, my eyes and ears were opened not only to the need of mass education, but also to the problem of the many dialects in China. In the far north I heard the clear inflection of the Peking speech which has been chosen as China's national language. When I came to Shantung, I heard the nasal twang. The Nankinese had added a high staccato tone, but lowered and flattened others. As we went down the Yangtse River to Shanghai, the sounds became more abbreviated and staccato, and the speech more rapid. As we visited Foochow, Amoy, Swatow and Hongkong, there were many changes in both consonants and vowels, and the tones multiplied, so that in Canton we heard eleven tones to the Peking four. Not only so, even we Chinese were not able to understand one another, and in some places had to have an American missionary interpret for us. In the province of Fukien alone, there are so many dialects that the people on one side of a mountain are not able to understand those on the other side. But I was greatly impressed with the large percentage of Bible-reading Christians in districts where the missionaries had used Romanized (English letters used to spell Chinese sounds) translations of the Bible and taught the people to read. In Amoy, every old lady, it seemed, brought her Bible to church and was able to find the references herself; whereas in most interior places, only a sprinkling of the educated could read at all. The Romanized, while good, only gave the uneducated a chance to read their own dialect. China needed the wide use of the government's National Phonetic System by which all could eventually learn to speak a standard dialect, and the illiterates might learn to read and write for themselves.

In some of the student centers, I lived in the dormitories with the students and had opportunities of doing personal work with them. After speaking, sometimes three times a day, I would give the students a chance for personal interviews. Lines of girls waited patiently outside my door for a chance to speak to me alone. Often I was busy until one and two o'clock at night; and then, too tired to take off my clothes and go to bed, I would just stretch out on the hard floor to rest. In this way I learned the importance of personal work and the hunger of the young people for the Word of God.

In each city we went to, plans for our meetings and the places where we were to stay were arranged by an interdenominational committee. We were often appointed to stay at the homes of missionaries or Chinese Christians whom we had never met or even

heard of before. A full program was always laid out for us, and
we had to hurry from the boat or train to meetings. At Hankow
I had to rush from the boat to the home of my hostess, and then
go at once to a meeting in the church. In the hurry, the name
and address of my hostess were mislaid. However, I remembered
to give a tract to the ricksha man who took me to the church.
When the meeting was over I did not know how to go back. As
I stood there in my dilemma, the same ricksha man came running.
Showing the tract, he asked, "Do you want me to take you back
again tonight?" The importance of tract distribution took on a
new value to me that night!

In Hongkong, I was impressed by the wealth of the Chinese,
the expensive feasts they gave, and the fine homes and clothes they
had. One day some girls invited me to their home on the peak
of the island where only the very rich live. They showed me the
view from their windows, and I looked down the steep mountain to
the beautiful green waters of Hongkong Bay, dotted with tiny
junks and great steamers from all over the world, and across to the
other side, to Kowloon City on the mainland.

The girls, wishing to give me a good time, kept passing around
chocolates, saying "Miss Tsai, have a sweet."

Suddenly a thought came to me and I spoke up, "Girls, why
don't you do something for the Lord with your money?"

One of them answered, "O Miss Tsai, we'd like to, but we
don't know how."

Another said, "I tell you. You be our missionary and we will
support you."

But I answered, "Why don't you start a home missionary
society and help evangelize China with Chinese missionaries?"

It was this unpremeditated conversation that acted like a
lighted match dropped into a pile of straw. Some of these girls
went to Kuling in 1918, where they helped organize the first
Chinese Home Missionary Society. Funds were raised, and a year
later six Chinese missionaries were sent out to the far southwestern
province of Yunnan.

So a jest stirred an ambition in me that bore fruit in leading me away from the high walls of my home to enter the wide fields of the Master's service. A resolve on the part of Mr. Milton Stewart released millions of dollars for world-wide evangelistic work. An unpremeditated conversation with some girls was a spark that started a fire of missionary zeal. Yet these were not chance happenings, but God moving "in a mysterious way His wonders to perform."

CHAPTER XIl

Out into the Byways

*T*HE MISSIONARIES entered the big city gates to build big churches and schools and hospitals and to form large communities like ours in Nanking. But they did more. A great pioneer work was done by Chinese and foreign missionaries going together in the countryside beyond, where modern ways had not penetrated and where life had gone unchanged for thousands of years.

I can see them riding the hardy Mongolian ponies over the desert wastes of China's great northwest, stopping at a caravansary to distribute tracts to the polyglot travelers from the remote corners of Central Asia. I see them seated in a springless cart, bumping along the dusty roads of the North, trying to reach a distant city by sunset. I can see them, legs doubled up, sitting astride patient donkeys that plod the steep hillsides to a hamlet four mountains and four valleys away. I see them propped up in a creaking wheelbarrow which is propelled along the rutty narrow path winding between flooded rice paddies; or getting off to relieve the wheelbarrow man and stretch their muscles, and talking to the blue-coated farmers on their way to market.

I can see them seated in a houseboat that is towed slowly along the banks of a canal, under high arched bridges where the village wives squat in a row, beating their clothes clean on the smooth stones. I can see them seated in a straw-roofed mud hut talking to the farmers' families while the dogs, cats and chickens pick up scraps around their feet. I can see them in heavy padded

92

Traveling by wheelbarrow in the country

Chinese clothes, resting for the night in some dirty inn while the curious natives stand around. I see them seated by a wayside teahouse at noon, munching a hot biscuit and surrounded by a crowd of curious children; or followed by a hooting mob who yell "foreign devil" and cast stones: I can see them in a little Jesus Chapel, in a narrow street of an isolated town, teaching the unlettered country folk. And I see the plain, semi-Chinese house, at the rear of the chapel, where a missionary family lives, or where two single ladies may live together. Missionaries of the cross, sojourning by faith in a foreign land.

I remember particularly a trip Miss Mabel Lee and I took into the country. We had to take everything we needed, and our equipment was assembled and packed the night before: clothes shoes, overshoes, toilet articles, a washbasin and bedding were wrapped up in quilts and roped inside a piece of yellow oilcloth. A kerosene stove, kitchen utensils, a dishpan, pails, tins of sugar, milk, bread and tea were packed in a big basket with a net that kept things in place. We took small wooden boxes for tables and stools, two camp cots, a large roll of hymn sheets, packages of tracts, pictures, Bibles and a guitar. We piled into the rickshas with all our baggage and were taken outside the city wall, where the houseboats were tied up along the banks of the canal. Bargaining was an important part of all business transactions, and it took knowledge of their ways and patience to find a fairly clean boat, and clinch the bargain for the day's trip.

The boatman and his family lived in the back of the boat, so we took the front. The woman rowed at the back, and the man poled from the side, and soon they took us past the cluttered market stalls, under the bridges and out into the country fields. It was spring and the winter wheat was beginning to beard. In some places the farmers were busy plowing with water buffaloes, and in others they were mending the mud-walled dikes that surrounded their little irregular fields, or fertilizing the soil with muck out of the ponds and canals.

In our part of China, as soon as the winter wheat was harvested, the fields were irrigated and planted for the summer rice crop. Along the narrow path that bordered the canal, the country people were bringing their products to the city. Donkeys laden with long sacks of grain jingled by, men carrying baskets of cabbage swung past, and wheelbarrows piled high with bundles of reeds for fuel creaked along. We passed white-washed brick houses with high walls, thatched mud huts, and red-walled wayside shrines. It was a long trip, but the air was bracing. We passed fields fragrant with yellow mustard, or sweet with the perfume of the bean flowers. Magpies and crows were building nests in the high trees, and the skylarks sung in the blue above our heads.

In the evening as we neared our destination, we passed great flocks of ducks swimming in our direction; the town we were going to is famous for them. It was already dark when we stepped off the gangplank at Chestnut Water, found carriers to take our baggage, and, heralded by a crowd of children, knocked at the door of the little street chapel. Elder East-Ear and his wife greeted us with delight. And while our things were set down in an empty room, Elder East-Ear lighted the little kerosene lamp, and we sat down together to exchange news while his wife took grass to fire the brick range and prepared us some noodle soup for supper.

Elder East-Ear, a tall man in rough country clothes, had a wrinkled face, scraggly whiskers and a nearly toothless smile; he was a hard worker, who loved the Lord and all His people. After we had eaten and had prayers, we went to bed.

The next morning we set up our own housekeeping with the things we had brought along, for there was no other furniture available. Neighbors began to drop in. The country women thought our box-stools and box-tables were wonderful, and one of them felt up Miss Lee's arm to see what she wore, and lifted up her dress to examine her underwear, exclaiming at everything and asking all kinds of questions. This was endured in a friendly way, for so it was meant. The Stones, a Christian family, who had a shop down the street, sent their eldest daughter with a gift of eggs. She brought two country girls with rosy cheeks and bangs hanging over their eyes with her, saying, "Here are two pupils for you."

I sat down on the bench near an old lady, and she launched into a long complicated story about her troubles, while I listened patiently. When she was finished, I said, "I've listened to you, now you listen to me." And I told her about Jesus. Only in this way could I win her attention. Elder and Mrs. East-Ear came in, saying, "We must go out and invite the people for the meeting this evening." Mr. East-Ear saddled his donkey and prepared to go to the farther places, while Mrs. East-Ear in a black head-kerchief, accompanied us to the nearer homes. As we stopped at one home on the street nearby, we heard the click of the mah-jongg ivories, and suddenly the door was closed in our faces. "Why don't they want us to come in?" asked Miss Lee. Mrs. East-Ear smiled at me as I answered, "If we go in with our books while they are gambling, they think we will bring bad luck and cause them to lose." (The words "lose" and "books" are both pronounced "shoo" in our part of China.) At another place we could tell from the way they said "We'll come, we'll come" that they didn't intend to do so at all. But at the third place the welcome was very sincere. The men of the family came in from the fields wiping their faces, and sat down to talk, while the children eyed us from a distance and the women served us poached eggs. They told us all that had happened during the past year.

We found other old friends; Mrs. Dai, a neat, intelligent woman, joined our party, and on the way told us a story: "Giving out tracts is certainly very good," she began. "Do you remember last year when we went to see Mrs. Wang who lives at Copper Well? You gave her some tracts and taught her 'I pray Thee, Lord Jesus.' Well, this year I went over there again and called in her home, and there the tracts were pasted up on her walls; and she could read them, too. 'How did you learn to read'? I asked her. 'My son taught me. When he came from school I'd ask him to read them to me. That is how I learned,' she said."

We arrived at a neat, white-washed thatched hut, and a middle-aged woman caught sight of us, dropped her broom and rushed toward us. "O Miss Tsai, Miss Lee." She grasped our hands in both of hers and exclaimed. "God has certainly sent you. My water buffalo is sick. I think it will die. Won't you come in and pray for it?" We did not laugh at this request, for the water buffalo was almost sacred to this Chinese peasant. They called him their ancestor and he slept in the house with them at night. It represented a fortune to this poor woman, for without it her fields could not be plowed. So we went in and prayed for the water buffalo, and it recovered.

We were back in the chapel by evening, and the crowd began to gather. We sat beside the early comers and tried to teach them to read a little tract. I sat down beside a young mother with a suckling child in her arms, and a toddler who was tugging at her coat. Half of her attention was on her children and half on what I said, but she repeated the words as I pointed them out to her and nodded her head as I explained the meaning. Finally the toddler nagged her so that she got up, and I went with her, continuing to teach her as I followed them around the chapel, "faint yet still pursuing"!

Miss Lee, who was very straightforward, caught sight of the women who had slammed the door in our faces, and said to them, "Unless you accept the Lord Jesus and ask Him to forgive your sins, He will shut the door of Heaven in your faces." She then brought out her guitar, hung up the large hymn sheets and we began to sing. Sing? No, not immediately. Each line had to be explained first and sung for them over and over again, while a few old hands joined in and helped us, each in her own tune and time. Though the harmony suffered, the good spirit made up for the musical defects and we knew it pleased the Lord.

I got up to give the message. I tried to use the words and experiences with which they were familiar, for they couldn't take in anything else. If I used a word outside their vocabulary, it was either lost entirely, or they gave it their own interpretation. For instance, once I used the Bible word for "porches," instead of their own word, and found on questioning a woman that she thought I said "wolves"! But the seed was sown and each year brought forth its own fruit, "first the seed, then the ear, then the full corn in the ear, for the Lord gives the increase."

CHAPTER XIII

Through the Golden Gate

B ETWEEN the eastern shores of my beloved land and the western coast of the beautiful continent of America, stretches the wide expanse of the Pacific Ocean. How I wish that the "Pacific" waters that break on the shores of each of these two great continents could preserve the peace that God meant to exist between us! Our two peoples have much in common, but only those who have crossed the ocean, or have known the people of both sides, can understand this and see that peace between America and China is one way to keep a bond of peace throughout the world. Our four hundred and fifty million people have been in political turmoil, as we have come out of our ages of seclusion and tried to adapt ourselves to the whirling modern world. Never, never could I have envisioned the conflict that is now going on between us! It would be useless to try to go over the political blunders that have brought this about. We can only say in the words of our Chinese people, "It is the will of Heaven"; for God has permitted it to come to pass that we may confess our evil ways, turn from them, and follow after His peace for all men everywhere, which is the peace of the cross.

Once a Chinese student in Shanghai asked me about America. "Why do you want to go to America?" I asked. "There isn't a student in Shanghai who doesn't want to go to America," he replied. This may be an exaggeration, but it certainly represents the spirit of my countrymen during the past fifty years, and it is partly a tribute to the missionaries who have come over, and partly a desire to see for themselves your fabulous material progress, or to have Ph. D. written after their names. I gladly welcomed the opportunity to accompany Miss Leaman on her furlough in 1921. While in Honolulu, we received a cable from some who were interested in missionary work, asking me to make a speaking tour of certain churches.

Our vessel passed the Golden Gate in the evening and the lights of San Francisco were my first glimpse of America. I noticed there was no confusion of shouting coolies on the dock as we tied up, and I was impressed by the orderly system of handling the baggage for custom's examination. In crowded China, there are generally a dozen people struggling for the same place; but here was room for all, and a strange Chinese girl named Christiana Tsai found true democracy and kindness wherever she went, whether from the taxi driver, the ticket agent, the Pullman conductor, or the cordial church members.

Miss Donaldina Cameron and Miss Tien-fu Wu, from the Presbyterian Mission for the Chinese in San Francisco, met us at the ship, just as they had met nearly every boat from China for many years. They took us to a nice apartment which had temporarily been lent to them for our use while the owner went to New York on a visit.

I would like to pay a tribute to these two women, now retired, for their great rescue work for hundreds of Chinese girls and little children caught in the snares of San Francisco's Chinatown. In her little room, Miss Cameron had a telephone by her bed, and at a call from the police, with whom she worked, she would rise from her bed at any hour of the night, go out and search for the person wanted, and then follow up the case in court, if necessary. While we were there, she received a call from the police asking her to find a Chinese girl who had been abducted to a house of prostitution. Miss Cameron went to the place, climbed up a fire escape, entered a room, took hold of the girl to lead her away, when suddenly, a sliding panel came between them and she was forced to loosen her hold and return empty-handed. But the case came up in court, and we went with Miss Cameron to the courthouse for the trial. She stood before the judge with her face pure as an angel's, accusing the Chinese owners of the brothel, while the lawyer for the defense, like a snarling wolf, tried to prove that the girl was there on legitimate business.

Everyone calls Miss Cameron "Lo-Mo" (Mother) and Miss Wu, "Auntie." A number of the girls said to us, "Lo-Mo and Auntie went down, as we Chinese say, to the depth of the sea, to the midst of the fiery furnace, into the dens of the lions, into the jaws of the wolves, to save us." Later, a large number of the girls married and were scattered to different states of America to witness for Christ.

On Sunday we went to the Chinese Church, where we met a zealous personal worker, "a hunting dog for the Lord." Miss Leaman mentioned by way of conversation that she regretted we hadn't had opportunity to speak to a certain Chinese family who had come over on the ship with us. After the service, we returned to our apartment, which, with all its modern conveniences, made us feel like babes lost in a mechanical woods. Miss Leaman had been away from the States for about twenty years, and I was a total stranger, so we had had no experience with modern conveniences. The first mechanical ogre we encountered was the self-service elevator. How were we to manipulate it? She tried to urge me, and I tried to persuade her to do it, but we both feared the terrible consequences of doing the wrong thing. So we climbed up and down the four flights of stairs! Our kind friends, Miss Cameron and Miss Wu, tried in every way to help us, but were not on hand and could not guess the extent of our ignorance. When the telephone rang, we were both frightened. "You answer it," I said. "No, you do," she said, for we were both sure we wouldn't be able to hear, and were too nervous to know what to say.

"There's no drinking water here," I said. "Do you think we can drink the tap water? Perhaps we had better boil some." So we boiled the water, as we had in China, not knowing the tap water was perfectly safe.

When mealtime came, and we were just sitting down to eat, there was a peremptory knocking at the door, making us jump. We found our zealous "hunting dog" friend at the door. "Here they are!" she cried. "I found them on the street and brought them up to see you. These are the Chinese you wanted to speak to on the ship, are they not?" Behind her was a bewildered Chinese family she had met and, with more zeal than tact, had taken in hand, hustling them up to call on us. Puzzled, they had followed, not knowing what it was all about. But they weren't the same people at all! We invited them in and they were pleased to find friends from China, though introduced in such a peculiar fashion. They proved to be from one of the leading Hongkong families whom I had met previously, and were really very happy to hear our witness and to find Christian friends over here. So the faithful "hunting dog" did bring in her quarry for the Lord after all.

While we were in San Francisco we heard many stories of the strange sects and cults that were so popular; but what distressed me most was to find that there was an American Buddhist temple in the city. We decided to see for ourselves what the place was like. Before we went in the door, we could smell the incense; stepping inside, we saw it was arranged like a Christian chapel, but up in front was a dais with a gilded Buddha on it; instead of a silk curtain, they had hung up over the idol a Chinese lady's embroidered skirt! A nun stood beside the dais, alternately striking the chimes and sounding the bell, while an American with shaven head, dressed in the orange robe of a Buddhist monk, was explaining to the audience that when Jesus was twelve years old, He hadn't gone to the temple at Jerusalem, but had gone to a Buddhist temple and received the teaching of Buddha. After the talk, they took up a collection, sang Buddhist prayers set to Christian hymn tunes, and at the close, the monk gave the benediction in the name of Buddha. This was sacrilegious to me. What a travesty to use Christian forms to worship an idol! I looked at the faces of the audience, and everyone of them was sad.

We hurried away, deeply distressed. It was missionaries who

had rescued me from Buddhism over in China, and now Buddhists were deceiving these gullible people over here! I had no words for my sorrow of heart. Outside on the bridge, I saw two women ahead of me, one short and dark and the other tall and thin. I recognized them as two from the audience, so I hurried up to the tall one and said, "Excuse me, please, but I am a Chinese girl who used to worship Buddha over in China, and I can tell you that you will never find peace that way. The only way to find peace is through the Lord Jesus Christ! I know, for that is how I found it."

The tall lady looked down at me and tears came to her eyes. "O little Chinese girl, please tell me where I can find peace! I am a relative of Robert Morrison. I have gone to all the churches over here, but I haven't found peace for my heart."

"Come to my house and we will talk about it," I said. "Here is my address—" But as I took a pencil and paper out to write, the short lady turned on me in fury, and shoved me back, nearly knocking me down. "Don't you try to convert us, you little Chinese girl! You have been deluded yourself by these missionaries." And she jerked the tall lady away, pulling her by force down the street, while I stood stunned. Robert Morrison's relative in a Buddhist temple in San Francisco! Incredible! The first Protestant missionary to China, who did a masterly translation of the Bible into Chinese, and his relative unable to find peace in America! It was he who, when an officer on the ship jokingly said, "So you are going to try to convert the heathen," had answered, "I can't, but God will." And now somebody was trying to convert his relative to Buddhism. I never saw her again, but the experience made an indelible impression on my mind, and I have prayed that she will find peace in knowing Jesus Christ.

All the time I was in America I rode on the crest of the wave. I was thrilled at all I saw, and everyone except the Buddhist woman on the bridge was kind to me. I saw the democratic spirit in action in all classes of people, and the great scope of Christian work everywhere.

In Pasadena, Mr. and Mrs. Milton Stewart were the first to call upon us, and they invited us to stay in their unpretentious home and served us with their own hands.

In Detroit, when I was to speak before the Presbyterian General Assembly, I hardly ate anything for three days. But as I mounted the platform, instead of seeing rows of long, severe faces, I looked at an audience all wreathed in smiles, and my fear left me.

After I spoke at the Moody Bible Institute in Chicago, the whole student body rose up and sang "Crown Him, Lord of All," and to my dying day I will never forget the inspiration that gave me.

In New York, I spoke to the prisoners at Sing Sing, and it was deeply satisfying that all I met had been given Testaments and professed a faith in Jesus. They lined up after the service to shake hands with me, and tears fell on my hand. Many said, "I'll meet you in Heaven."

At Northfield, Massachusetts, when I spoke to a group of working girls in D. L. Moody's home, they each donated an extra hour's pay for husking corn to raise money to buy me a victrola for country work.

In Washington when I shook hands with President Harding I gave him a box of ink which the Emperor of China had given my father, and he was so delighted he stopped to talk to me, and then ordered an attendant to show us around the White House.

At Leaman Place, in Pennsylvania, I remember with deep gratitude the helpful example of Miss Leaman's uncle, Dr. Henry Leaman, who for fifty-five years had been a practicing physician in Philadelphia. At six in the morning, without fail, he went to his room for prayer. Now he was blind, but still serene, and when I expressed my sympathy, he said, "The world is so full of evil, it is better not to see."

Several times when seated in a train, or on a trolley car, someone I did not know would slip a five-dollar bill into my hand, saying, "This is for your work in China."

At West Chester, Pennsylvania, and other places, I spoke to

Pray for China when you pull down the shade.

groups of children, and gave each child a Chinese brass coin with a hole in the center; I told them to fasten the coin to a window shade and remember that every evening when they pulled down the shade, it was morning in China, and to pray for the Chinese. Years later, during the Japanese war, some of those same children sent to a newspaper a letter suggesting that they tell the children of America whenever they pulled the shades down to remember to pray for the Chinese.

CHAPTER XIV

The Return of the Prodigal

NO ONE CAN RIDE the crest of the wave very long, as it is soon bound to topple and carry the swimmer down with it. It was not long before I passed through the deep waters. While I was still in America, Mother sold our house at Millstone Street, because it was too big and too difficult to keep in repair. She then moved to a smaller house at Fisherman's Wharf. This house was very gloomy and was quite a step down for us. She sent a cable which reached us in Japan, asking Miss Leaman to come and live with us, for she had given me to her for a goddaughter some years previously. Upon my return to Nanking I was very much shocked when the carriage deposited us at our new home, to find that our apartment was only a few rooms on the right of the main entrance. It seemed so public to one who had been used to living in the privacy of the inner courts, that I felt as if we were facing right out on the main street!

Mother looked especially well, and it was wonderful to see her and my family again. My own health had begun to fail, and many activities had to be given up. Then I received a great shock when my dear mother died suddenly the following year. I had gone to Kuling for a rest, leaving her well and happy; ten days later I received a telegram saying she had passed away. I hurried back for the funeral which I arranged to have carried out in accordance with her wishes, that is, with Christian dignity and simplicity, though some members of the family opposed this. She had told us that she did not want to be buried in Hangchow because she was now a Christian and wanted to be buried with the Christians. We buried her in a Christian hillside cemetery, in a plot adjoining that of Mr. Charles Leaman.

My Sixth Sister was a strict Buddhist, but she was impressed by the quiet, hopeful spirit of the ceremony. More than twenty-five years previously she had married into an immensely wealthy family in Nanking. Her father-in-law had held some of the same offices as my father, but he died soon and so did her husband, leaving her with three children, Enduring-Health, aged three, Bright-Cloud, aged two, and Enduring-Wealth, only six months. There were now three widows in this family, a grandmother, a mother and a daughter-in-law; so Enduring-Health was heir to a large part of the family fortune. With such a background, who could doubt the outcome? The three widows spoiled him when he was small, and could not control him when he grew older. Enduring-Health grew to be a vicious bully and a wild spendthrift. He sneered at their tears and protestations, and if they denied him money, rifled the family chests and made off with the valuables he found there. Thousands and thousands of dollars passed through his hands like water, all spent on wine, women and gambling.

One night during an orgy of gambling, he lost heavily, so he went home in the early morning hours determined to bully his grandmother until she gave him the money. He stalked into her bedroom before she had arisen, demanding, "Give me the pearl necklace that belongs to me. I want it now!"

Startled out of her sleep, she gasped, "What pearl necklace?"

"The one you said you were going to give me when I married," he answered.

"That pearl necklace!" she cried. "That is worth a fortune and we are keeping it for your bride!"

"I want it now! You can give her something else when the time comes," he stormed. "Hand it over quickly."

Outraged at his arrogance, she replied, "No, you shall never have it."

He sprang forward and slapped her on both cheeks, crying, "Are you going to give it to me, or not?" She screamed and Sixth

Sister heard her and rushed in, but he savagely pushed her away. The cook, who was passing by, heard the screams and he rushed in, too, carrying a bucket in his hands. He saw what was wrong and threw the bucket and its contents at Enduring-Health who ducked just in time. The cook, now mad with rage, shouted, "I'll rid the family of this scoundrel!" and threw a big carved chair at him, but the young man ducked again and ran away.

He left Nanking and went to Wusih, where the family owned several big stores, and tried to bully the managers into giving him money. At the same time he wrote letters home, threatening to break his brother's legs and make him impotent for life, so he could not be the family heir. He even hired cutthroats to lie in wait and maim Enduring-Wealth as he went to school, but this plot was found out and his brother was hidden away. Sixth Sister wrote to the store managers in Wusih, telling them not to give Enduring-Health any money, and also to the police, asking them to arrest him; but he was too cunning for them all, and escaped once more. Eighth Brother tried to trick him by asking him to the house for a game of chess, and his mother notified the police to surround the house. Enduring-Health came in and sat down to play the game, but soon suspecting a plot, got away, and so outwitted them again.

Next he went to a store manager, pointed a gun at him saying, "If you don't give me money, I'll shoot you." Some clerks set upon him and he had to flee. When poor Sixth Sister got this news, she was at her wit's end. There seemed to be only one course—have him arrested and put in jail, and she instructed the police accordingly. So Enduring-Health was finally arrested and imprisoned, and his mother put a notice in the paper publicly disowning him. This was a bitter day for her, and it was during this time that she brought Bright-Cloud and Enduring-Wealth to Fisherman's Wharf to live with us. Her Buddhist prayers and vegetarian vows had not helped her through this crisis, so she was more willing to listen as we told her how to find peace in Christ. But it took many weeks of patient teaching and explanation before she accepted Christ, and then broke her vegetarian vows. Later, Bright-Cloud and Enduring-Wealth accepted Christ and all three were baptized.

"Mother can you forgive me?"

As the trials multiplied, her faith deepened, and she committed Enduring-Health to the Lord and prayed faithfully for him.

Enduring-Health wrote asking me to speak to his mother and have him released from prison. Miss Leaman had sent him a Bible, and he quoted verses from it to show how repentant he was. When I suggested to the family that he be released, they all objected, saying, "We will have nothing to do with him. If he is let loose, you will have to take the whole responsibility." However, I decided to give him a second chance, and wrote to him that I would be his guarantor, if he would come home and live with me and promise to obey me. He agreed, and I secured his release.

The family was gathered together for morning prayers, and we were reading in Acts how Peter was delivered from the prison, when there was a commotion outside, the door burst open, and Enduring-Health stood before us. I took one look at his thin face, his long hair, the glare in his eyes. I knew that he was unchanged, that hatred still burned in his heart, and my own heart sank. "He hasn't repented! He fooled me! What shall I do?" I asked myself. His mother spoke to him, but he ignored her completely, addressing himself only to me. I showed him a room in my apartment which he could use, and made it clear that he wasn't to leave the house without my permission, and then only in my private ricksha.

Sixth Sister, Second Sister-in-law, and others blamed me. "Don't you see he hasn't changed a bit? He fooled you. Now we have a tiger in the house and there is no telling what will happen to us."

In his room, he proceeded to post slogans on the walls, "Death to my mother!" "Death to the manager!" "Kill my brother!" And in his rage he kicked the door to pieces. I tried to talk to him but he made no response, sitting sullenly and staring at the floor. His old amah said, "He is the worst scoundrel I ever saw. If this boy changes, all my village will believe in Jesus." I tried to find something for him to do, and asked him to copy some tracts for me. He did this but appeared to be just as stony as ever.

Then he started writing and composed some articles which

he sent to a newspaper for publication. He had an excellent, witty style, and the paper paid him well for all he sent in. So he found an occupation which kept him busy for some time. After two years he took university entrance examinations and passed at the head of the list. A change had come over him. Where he had been extravagant before, he now became miserly; where he had been idle, he became diligent; and where he had been wild, he now became quiet. Throughout these years he had never once spoken to his mother, so we knew he was still bitter and had no conviction of sin; but his mother never gave up praying for him.

Sometime after graduation he went to Hangchow on a study of the different colleges in that part of China. There he contracted typhoid fever, and was brought home dangerously ill. For weeks he lay growing thinner and weaker, and hovering at death's door. In this great extremity, God answered his mother's prayers, and opened his eyes to see that it was he who had sinned against his mother and brother, not they who had sinned against him. Like the prodigal son, he came to himself at last, and was overwhelmed by the magnitude of his sin. He asked for his mother. As she bent over him, he looked into her face for the first time in years, saw the suffering he had caused, and wept. "Mother, you loved me and cared for me, but I was a vicious dog who bit the hand that fed me, and hurt the only one who loved me. Can you forgive me?"

"You are my son," she said brokenly. "Of course, I can forgive you, but you must ask Jesus to forgive you, too. Only Jesus can take away your sin, and cleanse your heart."

"Yes," he replied, "I do want to ask Jesus to forgive me and be my Saviour. Will you pray for me?" As she prayed, the tears coursed down his thin cheeks. From that time on he began to get well, and had almost recovered when the amah ignorantly gave him some contaminated food, and he had a relapse. One day he asked for the pastor to come and baptize him. In a few days, Enduring-Health closed his eyes on this world, only to open them again as he crossed Heaven's portal and looked in the face of his Lord.

CHAPTER XV

Queen of the Dark Chamber

THE YEARS WE SPENT at Fisherman's Wharf saw the death of Mother, Second Brother and his wife, a cousin, a nephew, Enduring-Health, and the breakup of our family. Since my own health was poor, Miss Leaman decided to move to a house which we had previously built back of our chapel on Dye Factory Street. We hadn't had money to finish it at the time, so the neighbors called it "a leopard skin coat above and bare feet below" because the upstairs was finished with windows all around, but the downstairs was patched up with an odd assortment of latticed doors.

The years 1930-1937 spent on Dye Factory Street saw Miss Leaman accomplish her greatest work, and saw me go through the deepest waters of suffering. Miss Leaman realized a dream of her father's, envisioned fifty years before when he was toiling over study of the Chinese language, first for himself, and then trying to teach others to read the Bible. He dreamed of a simplified system of writing Chinese.

To us Chinese, the written character embodies the best of our culture. It is not just a mechanical symbol, expressing a sound, as the letters of the English alphabet are; but each character is a pictorial composite of various elementary ideas to form a new thought, and its written structure and style expresses our deepest thoughts and artistic attainment. Learning to read and write Chinese is so engrossing it becomes an end in itself. But—and here is the fatal flaw—it takes so much time to master the mere fundamentals that only the leisured few can ever enjoy it, while

111

the unlettered masses can only hope to learn to recognize a few characters at most. That means that even under a modern educational system only two out of ten can learn to read and write.

But Western culture introduced a new concept, namely, that writing is an indispensable means of communication for the masses, not a luxury for the privileged few. China's new leaders saw that our greatest educational need was to wipe out mass illiteracy among the four hundred and fifty million people and unify the confusion of dialects that exists all over China. Without accomplishing these reforms, China could never take its place in the modern world.

Korea has had such a system for a thousand years, and Japan had already wiped out illiteracy by similar means.

So the Chinese National Government formed a five-year plan by which it hoped to introduce the Peking dialect as a standard all over China, and carry on a program of mass education. They evolved a phonetic system to simplify the process of reading and writing. By combining thirty-seven symbols into words of not more than three symbols each, a person could write anything that was spoken in the colloquial language and read what was thus written.

To enlarge the usefulness of the system, each phonetic word was combined with its corresponding character in a parallel column so that anyone who had learned the phonetic could now also teach himself the character.

The phonetic beside the character is not only an accurate indication of the correct pronunciation of each of the nearly five thousand characters found in the Bible; it gives the correct tone as well. A very complicated character with the phonetic beside it is no harder to pronounce than a very simple one. Thus could be accomplished in a few weeks of intensive study what would require at least ten years in the old way.

And as for the missionaries, trying to master the hardest language on earth, as Chinese is said to be, the study of the phonetic teaches them accurate speech and accurate tones, which they rarely acquire otherwise. There are many jokes on the new missionaries for the many ridiculous mistakes they make in pronunciation and tones; but it is no joke when they continue to speak in a faulty way.

Miss Leaman saw in this program the possibility of printing the Bible with character and phonetic in parallel columns, and putting it into the hands of the millions of the common people. "A Bible in the hands of every man, woman and child in China" was her aim. The Bible read by the masses could do more to spread the gospel than any other means, while the strength of the Christian church depends to a great extent on the number of members who can read the Bible.

One day, while at dinner we were talking with a friend about the possibility of co-operating with the government in this mass-education program; the friend suddenly said, "I'll give you two thousand dollars to get it started."

It was a gift from Heaven, and Miss Leaman grasped it with both hands. At that time this sum in Chinese dollars was about six thousand, and would pay for the initial cost of launching the project. Miss Leaman obtained the services of an experienced printer and two apprentices, then secured a small office in Shanghai for them to use. All the work of finding the correct spelling and tones for the words, combining the character with the phonetic, designing the style of type, cutting the matrices, casting the type, typesetting, proofreading and printing, had to be carried on by correspondence between Nanking and Shanghai. She undertook to do the proofreading, and they did the mechanical labor of casting, typesetting and printing. The Bible Society agreed to do the publishing when it was done.

One lone woman with only two thousand dollars, undertook to have the whole Bible printed in character and phonetic for the people of China! It was a heroic task, but she was well qualified for it; she had a thorough knowledge of Chinese tones and common speech, an iron will, and a boundless faith in her task.

I was very much interested in this project, and prepared to help, but little knew what was ahead of me. One very cold morning on a visit to the mayor about some business, I noticed he had two nice stoves in his office, and wished I had one like them. When I returned home, I found my big room had been changed to a nice cozy one for the winter. I was no more than settled when two men appeared carrying a stove exactly like the ones I had seen in the mayor's office. Someone had sent it to me. How I enjoyed my nice cozy room and bright fire before retiring!

But I did not see it again for more than a year. In the morning I woke up to find the house apparently whirling around me, while daggers of light stabbed my eyes, and my body stiffened like a corpse in rigor mortis. I could not tell anyone what was the matter. I could only grunt and move my hand. Miss Leaman and the servants understood and nursed me faithfully. They hung dark curtains all around the walls to keep out the light, and covered my eyes with a black band. A woman was constantly at my side, though I lay there more dead than alive, unable to eat, unable to move for seventeen days, unable to speak for eight months, and unable to open my eyes for a year and a half.

Dr. Daniels, of the Presbyterian Mission, visited me frequently and did much for me, but at the end of one year, after all kinds of specialists had been called in for consultation, they announced that the case was hopeless, and advised notifying my family. My brothers, sisters, and friends prepared the coffin and the grave clothes, but Miss Leaman, who never gave up hope then or afterward, sent cables abroad asking for prayer, and hired a tailor to work upstairs to prepare summer clothes for me, while the family prepared my grave clothes downstairs. My family insisted on calling a famous Chinese doctor to examine me. He took my hand and said, "Miss Tsai, we all respect your good name, but you must know that the oil is dry and the lamp is going out. You cannot live longer than three days."

I lay on my bed too near death to have any pains, and saw a vision of a beautiful crown being lifted toward Heaven. I heard wonderful singing, and I thought to myself, "What a welcome!" But I heard a voice, saying, "No, not a welcome, only practice."

And I awoke to hear Miss Leaman praying and sobbing at my bedside. I had sunk to the lowest depths, but now began to recover.

The next day, Dr. Daniels sent a note, saying, "We have diagnosed the case. It is pellegra and beri-beri. No medicine will help, only forced feeding." (However, after sixteen long years of suffering, it was discovered that the basic cause of my trouble is malignant malaria in the marrow of my bones.) It was agony for us all to try and force the food down, for I had been so nauseated. As I got more nourishment, feeling came back and fiery pains began. My head seemed to be burning with fire, so for two years I had to have ice bags placed around it, while the women frequently gave me an alcohol rub and fanned me. The malaria in my bones was so terrible that even on winter nights, though the windows were open and the snow blowing in, I could scarcely stand the thinnest clothing, or bedding. Severe nausea made it difficult to eat and retain food. My mouth was sore, my hands black, and my knuckles cracked open to the bone. But I was able to take more food, and slowly God drew me up out of the depths and I returned to life again.

For a time, each step of progress was followed by a relapse. I'd get better, then the symptoms would return, and down I'd go again. But all through the darkness, the light of God's love never failed me. I could never tell all His great goodness to me, even if I had a thousand tongues, nor could I ever write of all His care and provision, even if, as the Chinese say, "The pen I hold could bloom," but I will tell of a few.

Across the Yangtse River about twenty miles away, was a little village. The farmers around there often heard the screaming and crying of an eighteen-year-old young woman, called Little-Beauty, who was beaten by her cruel husband and his family. One day after dark, Little-Beauty escaped from her home and hid somewhere in the fields. She trembled with fear as she heard the loud voices of her husband and her mother-in-law calling and cursing as they hunted for her. After midnight, everything was quiet and she started to run toward Nanking. Later she was brought to our home by a friend. She asked whether she might work in a hidden room, or just in the house, as she was afraid to go out, for fear her husband would find her. Thus she and I stayed together in the quiet of my curtained and darkened room.

She was a born nurse, and in her hours of rest she soon learned to read and write phonetic. A pile of books was filled with the nursing records she kept those days. She was most affectionate and thoughtful. I often felt her hot tears falling on my hand, and heard her say in a whispering voice, "O God of Heaven, when I am tired I can go out for a change, but when I come in, whether morning, noon, or at midnight, she is still lying here in the same position." For about eight months I was unable to talk much. I had to make my wishes known by a kind of grunt. She never had any difficulty in understanding me. Surely the Lord had put His love into her heart as day by day, month after month, and year after year, she nursed me with never a sign of murmuring or of complaint.

Since my room had to be kept quiet and dark, the rats started to have a good time. They played and danced around me. They liked to crawl up the curtain and jump to the head of my bed, then walk from my shoulder to my hand. For several mornings, before daybreak, I heard a tiny bell jingling outside my window. The little bell bothered me, and the woman went down to see what it was. They found a beautiful pure white Persian cat, with a big, bushy tail and affectionate eyes, with a bell tied around its neck. Naturally, we did not want to keep anyone's pet. Miss Leaman tied a pink tract to the cat's neck and sent her off. In a little while she came back but the tract was gone. Miss Leaman tied another tract to her neck and sent her off again. Thus our pussy evangelist carried quite a number of tracts to different homes. Before long, she settled down and refused to leave us. You can imagine how rapidly the rats disappeared when White Queen walked around the house.

Outside my windows was a yard with a small peach tree and a mulberry tree. During the long summer days, the reflection

White Queen, the pussy evangelist

from this open space was unusually bright and hot. Two months after I was taken sick, a kind friend ordered three trees planted a few yards away from my windows, and before long, all around the yard, about thirty trees grew up in addition to the original three. If we had carefully planned where to plant them, we could not have selected such good places. They grew so quickly that three years later the once empty yard became a little forest. The tops of the branches and the beautiful leaves touched each other, and formed a big parasol covering the entire space. Friends often spoke of the view from my windows, the beautiful shade and the sunlight filtering through, and said, "It is a miracle."

Our old gateman who had been with our family for forty years never would answer me when I asked him to accept Jesus. He would only stand there without a word, neither refusing nor accepting. But on the day he heard the Chinese doctor say I had only three days to live, he ran over and sought the pastor, saying, "I want to go along with Miss Seven. I want to confess my sins and go with her." So at last in this my extremity he turned to the Lord. Now I can say from the depths of my heart, "My extremity has been God's opportunity."

During my illness a kind friend asked me whether I were lonely and tired spending my days in a darkened room. "Oh, no!" I answered, "the Lord is my constant Companion and real Friend. I am queen of this dark chamber and He is my King of Light!"

CHAPTER XVI

The Light That Never Failed

*D*URING MY LONG ILLNESS, did Miss Leaman stop her work on the phonetic Bible to care for me? Oh, no! If you think that, you don't know my godmother, Mary Leaman. Difficulties to her were only evidence of the supreme importance of her task, and they were faced calmly but with immovable determination. As she helped me out of the valley of the shadow of death with her constant prayers, her loving care, and her iron will, so she went ahead with her self-imposed task of translation with equal dedication. Perhaps many imagine her as a strong, active, healthy woman. She suffered from a spinal injury which left her in constant pain and weakness, so she rarely could go out. In her spare time, after taking care of my many needs, she would sit in a reclining chair, with a typewriter beside her and a reading table on her knees, and work into the early hours of the morning. In this way, she carried on her wide correspondence and the endless, exacting labor of proofreading. She also trained many students and teachers to help with the proofreading, and enlisted the services of anyone she could interest in the labor. She taught the servants to read and used them for demonstration purposes. Miss Helen Struthers spent two years helping with publishing and promotion.

There was a Mission Phonetic Promotion Committee in Shanghai who also backed her, and numerous missionaries who had the vision and made the effort to teach the common people to read by this method. Curiously enough, neither the illiterate masses, nor the literates, nor the missionaries as a whole, welcomed the opportunity or believed in this method. They were too wedded to using the character, too doubtful of the possibilities of adapting the Peking spellings to the local dialects, and too easily discouraged by the difficulties of launching a new system. Many started full of enthusiasm, and stopped quickly when they met the apathetic response of the people; for illiterates will take great pride in knowing a few characters, but will resist any new ideas, especially what seems like a foreign language to them.

What seemed so easy to a Westerner, used to a phonetic system of spelling, was extremely difficult to the mind-set of my people. The Chinese were used to learning to recognize each character by memory alone; and though they spoke in tones, they never recognized them as tones, thinking of them only as different words. With their minds directed toward the recognition of the character more than understanding of the subject, they often missed the meaning entirely unless it was put in extremely simple form. In fact, the difficulties of this program were so many that without the government to enforce it, individuals could do very little. But when a dull, stupid woman was coaxed over the hurdles of spelling, and the light of the meaning from some tract or Bible verse illuminated her mind, it so stimulated her emotions and awakened her dormant reasoning power that she was transformed. When she realized that she was reading Chinese (not English as they ignorantly supposed at first), that she could write her own letters; and when the wonders of God's Word dawned on her mind, she became entranced with the Bible and glowed with a new-found intelligence. An old lady corrected a preacher for mispronouncing a word, saying, "In my Bible [the Phonetic] that word is pronounced this way." And sure enough, she was right and he was wrong!

The Book of Jonah was the first to be finished and printed, and it was followed by others. So we had several textbooks for a group of country children who came in to study in our chapel. The country people are very busy most of the year, but in the winter, after the China New Year, they have time to study, and that is when we have to work the hardest. Children learn much more quickly than adults, and these children learned to spell and read and write very well in six weeks, so we sent them home with their books and told them to continue with their reading and try to teach others. When they got home they were proud of their new-found education and often sent us postcards written in phonetic. Later, a farmer from their part of the country came in to see us, his face full of smiles, bringing a "thank you" gift of eggs and puffed rice, and a story to tell.

"This phonetic," he began, "is a living treasure. My daughter, Precious Pearl, was in your short-term school this year. When she came home, she amazed us all by reading the Bible to us and keeping our accounts as well! So our neighbors used to drop in and ask to hear her read.

" 'This is nothing short of a miracle,' one said. 'This child did not know one character before. Now she can read the Bible. Who ever heard anything like that?' Another said, 'Maybe she isn't reading correctly. Let's call in one of the big boys who has been to school to test her.' So they called in one of the boys and gave him a Bible to look at and asked her to read from hers. She read every word correctly. That boy had studied five years and couldn't read as well as she did. Now when our people find some new and difficult character, they come to her, and if there is phonetic beside it, she can tell what it is. So they all call her 'Little Dictionary.' "

The story of the painter and the carpenter is another interesting case. We had hired a man to paint our house. This man was an earnest Christian, a diligent worker, but an illiterate. He was greatly impressed the first day on attending our morning prayers, to see the cook, the washwoman and the coolie each with a New Testament in hand, take turns reading the lesson. Afterward, they urged him to learn the phonetic, too; he stood there, face red, ears burning, unable to say a word. He was a stutterer! But he wanted to learn. So it was wonderful to see him in his spare

Little Field   Old High   Little King

Three servants reading the Bible in phonetic

time, seated on a stone, a page grasped in both hands, spelling, "b-b-b-b—ah bbah, p-p-p—ah ppah, m-m-m—ah mah, d-d-d—ah dah." Even standing on the ladder busily painting, he kept on repeating, "Bah, pah, mah, dah," and while he was working, he would stop, lay down his brush, take up his book, and hunt up some new word.

One day he told us that the wood in some of the doors and windows was rotten, and we should get a carpenter to fix them before painting. The carpenter arrived, but had hardly begun work when the painter came over and persuaded him to study phonetic. When the carpenter opened his mouth to pronounce the sounds, they both guffawed. Everybody came around to see what the joke was. "He is a stutterer, too," said the painter. But the stuttering teacher and the stuttering student were encouraged, rather than discouraged, by their mutual handicap. They were often seen under the trees on a big stone, each with his book, drinking tea together, and reading with great gusto.

The government plan for the phonetic was now in full swing. All primary school textbooks contained it, and many public notices as well. The mayor of one city ordered the people to attend public classes to learn the phonetic, but few enrolled. "We are too busy," they said. So the mayor stationed teachers at the city gates to examine all the people entering the city in the phonetic, and to allow only those who could read to enter. This solved the problem, and the classes were well attended, because the country people all needed to come into the city to do business.

In Nanking, in June, 1937, the Board of Education called a conference of one hundred delegates from all over China for a month's training in methods of teaching phonetic to the people. The head of the Department of Mass Education knew of Miss Leaman's work, and asked her to send some phonetic pupils to demonstrate to the delegates. She got in contact with a Miss Garden, an old Chinese friend of ours, who had started evangelistic work in the country about twenty miles south of Nanking. This woman had contributed her own savings to build a little chapel and she personally helped the masons and carpenters. She was teaching a class of boys and girls to read phonetic. They worked all day, carrying vegetables, digging edible wild plants on the hills, pulling rickshas, keeping buffaloes, or gathering fuel, and came every evening for a half-hour class in phonetic. Miss Garden now hired two carriages and told her pupils they were going on a trip into the city with her. They squeezed into the carriages just as they were, the boys carrying books in their hands, and the girls, heads tied up in black kerchiefs, with their books in baskets. The children thought the trip was a great lark, and stared wide-eyed at the wonders of the capital. Miss Leaman met them and they drove in through the imposing gates of the Department of Education.

But their eyes opened wider as they were taken into the great assembly hall, and up to the platform in front, where they saw the great company of educators. But they were too simple to be frightened, and they went through all the tests with flying colors.

The delegates were invited to test the children, so one of them came forward, picked up one of their books, opened it at random, and asked a child to read. He did so, successfully. Then another delegate came forward with a book of his own containing phonetic, and gave it to one of the boys to read. Though he had never seen that book before, he was able to read the words. When a third educator pointed to an inscription on the wall, and asked one of the girls to read it, she was able to do so. This demonstration made a great impression on the educators. They awarded Miss Leaman a set of phonetic records prepared by Dr. Y. R. Chao, an authority on phonetic, and asked us to prepare a message on the value of the phonetic, to be broadcast over the Central Broadcasting Station. I was just well enough then to dictate the message, and later dictated for publication several booklets on the importance of the phonetic.

CHAPTER XVII

Wanderings in the Wilderness

NANKING was the capital of China from 1927 to 1937, and during those years the population mushroomed from two hundred thousand to a million. Wide streets were cut through the city and country; bus service was started; numerous government buildings sprang up; and the city was thronged with strangers from all over China and all over the world. The government was working feverishly to unify China, reform its laws and educational system, and modernize its army, all of which were colossal tasks.

But there were enemies without as well as within. A great nation on the other shore of the Yellow Sea knew the strategic importance of China to her own ambitions, and had plans to conquer it. While the Chinese government was trying to reform the national economy, the Japanese were encroaching in the North, biting it off piece by piece. Could China in these short years become strong enough to defend herself? Because it looked as if she might, the Japanese decided not to take the chance.

In the summer of 1937, Japan struck first north of Peking, and then at Shanghai on the central coast. There was nothing to do but hold them off at Shanghai while the government was evacuated to the mountain fastness of West China, and then draw them in until they bogged down in the primitive maze of the interior. So, as the Japanese army advanced from the coast, the people fled to the west. All government personnel and their dependents were ordered to leave, and with them went the young,

125

Mountains of West China

the rich, the patriotic and the intelligentsia; behind stayed the poor, the old, and women and children. Higher educational institutions moved en masse across those thousands of miles. Modern factories were dismantled and carried piece by piece overland. Nanking was a bottleneck through which millions of frantic refugees tried to pour, for they were forced to make a choice between staying to suffer the terrors of a Japanese occupation, or fleeing across the jigsaw paths of the interior. The few railroads, bus lines and steamships could accommodate only one out of a hundred of those who wanted to go. I cannot describe that great exodus but I will tell you a little of God's wondrous care for His children in those days, both for those who went and those who stayed.

Miss Arrow and Miss Willow, two Chinese evangelists, had decided to go by train to the country south of Nanking. When they got to the railroad station, it was crowded with thousands of struggling people, trying to get on an already packed train. They discovered that some baggage had been left behind, and Miss Arrow went back to get it. She did not find it, and before she returned, the train had gone, taking Miss Willow, the money, and the rest of the baggage. Miss Arrow stood there in the seething crowd, five dollars in one hand, and a small handbag containing a change of clothing in the other. Another train was going south, but it was already jammed and people were climbing through the windows to the coach tops. There seemed no hope at all of getting even standing room. As she stood there, a stranger asked her, "Do you want a seat on that train?"

"Certainly," she said, "can you get me one?"

"Come with me," he replied, and took her to a coach which had been reserved for the families of government officials. She was thrilled to get a seat, but later dismayed to find that the train did not stop at the appointed place, but went on far beyond it to a strange town where everybody got off. Here, too, the Lord provided! One of the families on the train hired a house boat and invited her to join them for the next stretch of the journey. When they parted at the second town, she found a

Christian chapel where she stayed and then joined another Christian group who were going farther on. Thus step by step she went west, where she found a home and work to do.

Miss Garden's wanderings were similar but even more prolonged. She went from town to town throughout inland China, carrying her little satchel and a few dollars. Everywhere she went she found little Christian chapels and mission stations where she was entertained, and directed by devoted Christians who were mostly members of the China Inland Mission. She slept on straw on the floor, washed at the well, ate the simple food they provided, preached at the evangelistic services, taught Bible classes, and joined new groups of refugees who went west as the news came that the Japanese were approaching. They traveled by houseboat, wheelbarrow, or donkey, or on foot all through the picturesque hill country of central and southwest China. The Christians of the interior welcomed her and asked her to preach to the crowds that passed along, so the opportunities for witnessing were unlimited. For eight years, from the beginning of the war in 1937, she wandered through ten provinces, preaching, teaching and witnessing with no other means of support than what she received as she went along; she did not return to Nanking till the war was over in 1945. She told us that until then she had no idea of the far-flung work of the China Inland Mission and their sacrificial service and hospitality to the people of China in those days.

There was old Mrs. Wang who left with her family to hide in the country not far from Nanking. They had rented the middle house in a row of three in a little hamlet. The young women in the party hid under the boards of the floor all day to escape the bestial lust of the roving Japanese soldiers. One day they saw a Japanese soldier approach, and the girls hid while the older ones watched and prayed. The soldier entered the first house and came out, but just as he started to enter the middle house, a dog sprang at him and he turned to chase it away, so that he skipped the middle house and went to the third.

Old Mrs. Chen and her family were too poor to hire rickshas

to get out of the city, so they remained at home. Some Japanese soldiers entered their house, saw the men standing in the court-yard and fired, killing them all, and left. She and her daughter-in-law, the only ones left, witnessed the shooting and were frantic. What could two helpless women do all alone? In their terror they jumped into the well. While they were struggling in the water, another Japanese soldier entered, heard the noise, and looked down the well at them. He smiled at them and indicated that they were not to fear. Then he let down a rope, drew them out, got them some dry clothes and gave them money. When they tried to express their gratitude, he said simply, "I am a Christian."

An American woman missionary with sublime courage, walked out on the streets time and again when the atrocities were at their worst, and gathered up screaming women who knelt and implored her help. She brought them to Ginling Women's College where she and a band of heroic friends turned the beautiful buildings into a huge refugee camp, using the protection of the American flag. For five months they fed and protected the women against outrage. During those months tens of thousands of refugees were housed in several other such refugee camps, operated by mission-aries. The women of Nanking used to say, "It was that American missionary who saved us Nanking people. We thought she was Christ Himself."

As for Miss Leaman and me, who had lived in the shadow of Japan's aggressive designs for many years, and had seen the tiger appeased again and again, we never knew just when it would spring. We went on with our lives just as usual, hoping for the best. Miss Leaman was trying to finish the printing of the Bible and at the same time shield me from worry. I did not know what was happening until a Chinese friend came into my room one day to tell me of the mass exodus and to urge us to go to the foreign concession in Shanghai, which the Japanese had not attacked at that time.

We decided to pack and leave at the earliest opportunity. Mr. Wang, our printer, spent three days at the railroad station before

he succeeded in getting us a first-class compartment. Later the conductor kindly allowed our three women servants to stay in the
room with us instead of putting them in third class. Had they
gone third class, they would have had to wait for the next train,
and would surely have been lost in the mêlée. They were simple
country people who had never been on a train before, and one
of them, whom we called Little-King, kept moaning all night long,
"O my mother! O my mother! What is going to happen to us?
How can we all live in this little room?"

Suddenly, for the first time, a terrible thought occurred to
me, and I said, "Miss Leaman, where are we going to live in
Shanghai?"

"I don't know, dear," she answered; "the Lord will provide."
The train was on time when we arrived in Shanghai, and Miss
Leaman looking out of the window, cried, "There is Joy-Bell to
meet us!" There she stood among the thronging masses, and a
nurse with a wheel chair was with her. We were expecting
Joy-Bell for we had sent a telegram asking her to meet us. What
we did not know was that she had not received the wire, but in
her morning devotional watch, she had been guided to go down
and meet that train. And now our car door stopped at the very
spot where she was standing. As we pushed through the frantic
crowds, another miracle appeared—two empty taxis waiting at the
curb.

"There are mountains and oceans of people, all trying to find
a place to live here in Shanghai," Joy-Bell told us. "There is no
use trying to hunt for a place today. You had better get a room
in a hospital for the present." But a hospital room was small for
us five, and the price was too high, so we telephoned Eighth
Brother to find us a place.

"There isn't a square foot of empty space in Shanghai!" he
exclaimed.

"Try your best," we urged. So he sent his son Ever-Cheer
and daughter-in-law Bright-Cloud to find us a room. They walked
the streets all morning but found nothing. By noon they were

Three refugees in a pedicab in Shanghai

hot and tired, and they sat down to eat in a little Russian restaurant on the Street of the Coiled-Dragon. Just across the street
was a row of brick houses. While they were eating, a Russian
woman appeared and pasted a tiny square of paper, the size of
a calling card, on the door of one house.

"Let's see what it is;" said Bright-Cloud; "it might be a room."
They ran across the street and found it was notice of a room to
rent! They had seen it in the nick of time, for other room-
hunters were prowling the streets! The woman was still outside
when they appeared at the door, and she took them upstairs to
see the room which had a bath adjoining. It was ideal for our
purposes! So Bright-Cloud stayed in the room to hold it from
room-hunters who followed them, while Ever-Cheer went to
telephone us. "We've found a room for you, but if we leave the

house now, we'll lose it," he said. "Just come over to this address as quickly as you can."

Joyfully we entered our new home in exile and unpacked our things, just seven hours after our arrival. "Get Miss Leaman some fresh clothes out of her trunk," I told Little-King.

When she opened the trunk she cried out, "It's full of phonetic books. There isn't a piece of clothing here."

"What!" I cried, "didn't you pack her clothes?'

"She said to pack these phonetic books because she needed them," was the answer.

"Well, Little-King, you will have to lend her a suit of your own clothes till we make some new ones," I said.

CHAPTER XVIII

Three More Sheep

*T*HE FOREIGN CONCESSIONS in Shanghai were sand-
wiched between the old and new Chinese cities. Here Shanghai had its British and American quarter, French quarter, Japanese
quarter, Russian quarter, and later its Jewish quarter. The aliens
were only a sprinkling in the Chinese population that now over-
flowed every corner and swelled the city to three times its normal
number because of incoming refugees. Though Shanghai's foreign concessions were a thorn in the flesh of the patriotic student
class who resented China's lack of sovereignty, they were a haven
of refuge to the wealthy people who found security in their international control. During the first part of the war, from 1937
to 1941, Shanghai became a vast refugee camp.

We lived in the French concession, but there were very few
French living there. The largest foreign element around us were
the white Russians who had fled here after the Russian Revolution
and it had become the Russian quarter. Around the corner was
Avenue Joffre which was then commonly known as "Little Mos-
cow Boulevard" because of the Russian shops that lined the street
and the many Russian people who strolled on its sidewalks.

Scarcely a week after we moved there, the Japanese siege of
Shanghai began, and though no bombs fell in the concessions, the
Japanese and Chinese fired at each other across this area. The
screaming of the shells and the roaring of the artillery never ceased
until Shanghai fell to Japan three months later.

Miss Leaman went on with the proofreading of the phonetic

Bible. Some time before she had all the printing apparatus moved from Shanghai to Nanking; when we left Nanking it had to be moved up the river to the buildings of the Religious Tract Society, in Hankow, where it remained intact for the duration. Had it been left in the original Shanghai office, which was in the Japanese quarter, or in Nanking, it would have been destroyed and Miss Leaman's labor and capital lost.

Our landlady Olga was a white Russian as were most of the other occupants of the house. The afternoon we arrived she was away playing mah-jongg, and the Chinese servant known as "Boy" showed us the room. In the evening Olga clattered upstairs in her high heeled shoes and came to visit us. She was an attractive young woman, dressed very stylishly and she spoke in broken English, "You are the new guests, Miss Leaman and Miss Tsai, yes? See I bring you a sheet and some plates. Please you use them."

"Thank you very much. You are our landlady, I suppose. What is your name?"

"Please, my name is Olga. You like to play mah-jongg with me?"

"No, we don't play mah-jongg. We are Christians."

"Not play mah-jongg! Why not?" and she turned away and click-clacked down the stairs.

In a few days she came back. "Please you pay me rent now?"

"But we paid you rent when we took the room."

"No, no, not this month. Next month. I play mah-jongg and lose very much money. Please you pay me now."

So whenever Olga came to see us it was either to ask us to play mah-jongg or to borrow money. The rest of the time, though we could not see her, we heard her yelling downstairs, "Bo-o-oy! Come here!" or "Mimi, [her dog] where are you?" When she lost at mah-jongg the glasses, plates, forks and spoons would begin to crash, and the dog would yelp, as Olga beat her and chased her into the hall. She quarreled with all the roomers except us. I could often hear doors slamming and angry voices and screams, for they often came to blows. Nearly every day the police came to the house to investigate the quarreling and fighting. Olga had been living with a Swedish man named Nils for seven years, though they were not married. He worked as a guard in the municipal jail during the day. When she got mad at him, the plates and glass and silver crashed. Often they went out for dances and returned in the early hours of the morning, singing noisily, too drunk to go to their own room. Our servants going down in the morning would stumble over them sleeping on the stairs.

The boy, who had a speech difficulty, used to come upstairs and pour out his woes to me because I was a Chinese. "Missy throw her shoes and stockings on the floor and tell me to pick them up. She has plenty dresses, but she no like them. She roll them up and throw them in the closet."

Olga's mother, sister, nephew and niece came down from Port Arthur, and they all slept in one room under mine. Olga often fought with them, grabbing her screaming niece by the hair; the mother and nephew jumped on Olga, and down went the table, chairs, Olga, niece and nephew together.

One day one of the tenants had a birthday and invited Olga to play mah jong with her. They played continuously for forty-eight hours, and Olga lost two hundred dollars. To pay the debt she sublet her own room, and tried to move a heavy trunk. In so doing she injured herself severely. For months she was so weak she could hardly drag herself around. One day she came upstairs to see us and sat down groaning on the chair to tell us the doctor said she must have an expensive operation. Miss Leaman had often talked to her about Jesus and now urged her to pray for herself. So Olga went to her room, got on her knees, and prayed, "Dear God, I am a naughty, naughty girl. Please, You make me well and I promise You I will never, never play mah-jongg again. And I won't drink, or dance, or quarrel any more." Immediately she felt well inside. Nils came home that night saying he had made arrangements for her to go to the hospital.

"No, no, Nils. I tell you good news. I am not sick any more."

"Nonsense! The doctor said you could not get well without an operation."

"Please, Nils. I don't need an operation. Jesus made me well." And she refused to go, for she really was well again. As soon as she could, she hurried up to our room, and though we were entertaining company, she could not wait to tell us the news of the miracle.

Olga kept her promise, for she was a changed woman after that. The house became quiet at last. She would often come upstairs to pray and read the Bible. She prayed in a simple childlike way, "Father, You know I may fall down. Please You pick me up." One day while reading Porverbs her conscience smote her and she told us, "The Bible tell me, 'You lazy little thing! Go look at that ant. It works all summer to get ready for the winter.'" So she pulled her discarded dresses out of the closet and started to learn to sew for herself.

She went to pay her gambling debts, too. As she stood in the doorway of the gambling room, she feared to go in lest she be tempted again; but when she looked at the greedy faces and trembling hands of the gamblers, a surge of relief went through her that she was delivered from that old slavery, and she praised God for the new life she had found.

Now she wanted to help her boy, and asked Miss Leaman to teach him. "Please you teach him. I have a new heart and I want him to have a new one, too. The Bible has many lovely things and I want him to read them."

But this new way of life did not please Nils, who said, "You say don't dance, don't smoke, don't drink! I work in jail all day and now you make my home a jail too."

However, Olga had learned to go to God in prayer, so she prayed, "Please, Father, I love Nils. I want him to go the same road with me. But if You wish him to leave me, all right. Please You put Your wishes in our hearts." And God answered her prayer, for one day Nils had a holiday, took her to a church, and they were married.

Our house was full of noises of all kinds. An educated Chinese woman rented one of the rooms downstairs. Her husband had cast her off and she tried to find comfort in Buddhism. Every morning at daybreak, she would raise her voice and loudly chant her prayers. Most of the other roomers caroused at night, and they complained that she disturbed their rest in the morning. We spoke to her often of the comfort of Christianity, but she showed no interest. Finally, one day she told us that she had decided to go to the West and find her husband, so we gave her a Bible as a parting gift. Some months later we received the following letter from her:

> Miss Tsai and Miss Leaman:
>
> I have not seen you for a long time, but I often think of you. After I left Shanghai and went to find my husband, I was arrested at Hankow for a spy and put in jail, where I will have to stay six months. Here I had nothing to do so I read the Bible you gave to me, and it has brought the true peace into my heart. The more I read the more wonderful it becomes, and I like to tell the other prisoners about it, too. The jailers allow me to read the Bible to these people. Thank you so much for this wonderful gift.

Her next letter told us that she had been released from jail and found her husband, and that they were reunited.

Another tenant was a Jewish woman, a refugee from Europe, whom we heard crying much of the time. Her terrible experiences and sorrows had undermined her health and left her mentally unbalanced, and her husband's scolding made her worse. She was sent to a hospital and put in a strait jacket. After a while she returned, only to break down again. She refused to listen to any words about Christ, and when she visited us during the Passover Week, she even refused to drink a glass of water in our room. However, after a while she began to read a Bible we had given her. These Words of Life brought comfort to her heart, and she found peace and quiet at last. Some time afterward she had an opportunity to go to America, and she took her Bible with her, writing us that she was continuing to read it every day and find comfort in it.

Three lost sheep! A refugee Russian, a refugee Chinese, and a refugee Jewess! But the Good Shepherd found them all, and brought them safely into His fold.

CHAPTER XIX

Clouds and Sunshine

CLOUDS MAY GATHER over our home in times of sickness or bereavement; but the influence of a sweet Christian character shines through the clouds with a golden radiance, bringing a lasting blessing to those who remain. The story of my sister-in-law, Class-Leader, demonstrates this.

Living in Shanghai, we frequently saw Eighth Brother and his family. His eldest son, Ever-Cheer, was married to Bright-Cloud; his daughter, Ever-Wise was a nurse, and his younger son, Ever-Famous, a student in college. As for his wife, Class-Leader, she was as bright and cheerful as a ray of sunshine, and we all loved her.

One afternoon in autumn she came over to have a brief chat with me and then left with a cheery good-by, walking away through the evening shadows. Neither of us dreamed that this would be our last visit together. A few days later she was taken sick and was sent to the hospital.

On Thanksgiving Day, Eighth Brother came to see me; although he tried to hide it, I knew he realized Class-Leader would soon leave us. All day long, my heart was fixed in prayer that Class-Leader's homegoing might prove a blessing to the ones she left behind. That afternoon at the hospital, the north wind rattling the window panes of the little room was the only sound as her loved ones gathered round her bedside, intently watching her every move. About sunset Class-Leader opened her eyes for the first time in her illness and taking hold of Bright-Cloud's hand

139

pointed upward exclaiming, "What a wonderful place! What a beautiful sight! Can you see it?"

In a little while she left us and went to that beautiful place to be greeted by her heavenly Father. It was all joy for her, but my brother had lost his best companion and her children had lost their sympathetic mother. They missed her at every turn. Ever-Wise told me, "When I woke next morning I saw nothing but my *white mourning shoes and my white mourning dress before me!"

Yet Class-Leader's voice was not still. She continued to speak to her family, this time through her will: her last request being that she be buried wearing her golden cross and with her Bible by her side. This impressed Ever-Famous, who now decided to read his Bible every day, and often came and read at my bedside. But when Christmas time came around the emptiness in his house seemed unbearable. There could be no party this year for there was no mother to entertain his non-Christian friends, no one to tell them the Christmas story, serve them tea and cakes, and give them gifts. But here Ever-Famous, who was more than economical, thought of a very fitting way to celebrate instead. He took his carefully hoarded savings and bought twenty Bibles to give his non-Christian friends in memory of his mother. Then he wrote the name of each friend on the flyleaf and took the Bibles to their homes.

One friend, Hidden-Treasure, became especially interested, and they used to spend hours in Bible study and prayer together. Afterward she became a Christian, and in a short time they became engaged and now they are happily married. So the sweet faith of Class-Leader continued to be a blessing to her son, leading him to a Christian wife and home.

Nor was this the only blessing her last words bequeathed, for on my birthday, Ever-Famous burst into my room, his face all

---

* White is the color for mourning in China.

aglow with good news. "Auntie Seven, what do you think our old servant, Old-High, said to us today?"

"I can't guess. Tell me."

"She said, 'I can never forget the smile on my tai-tai's* face before she died and her words, "What a beautiful place! What a wonderful sight! Can you see it?" ring in my ears day and night. She used to urge me to believe, but my heart was hard and sinful, and I made her sad by refusing. Now I want to see that beautiful place, too. For twenty years I have refused Jesus, but now I believe and want to be baptized.'"

After Ever-Famous had left, Little-King, who was in the room at the time, said to me, "Miss Seven, I've been with you seven years and I have believed in my heart for a long time. Now I want to confess Jesus before others. May I be baptized with Old-High?"

Little-Field, our washwoman, soon heard the news and she too, came to me eagerly, saying, "You know, I believe Jesus and I want to be baptized too."

So one afternoon the three women servants gathered around my bed for three hours of instruction and prayer for the coming service. I was thrilled by the marvelous change in the three women. They were full of joy and had many experiences to relate, especially Old-High. She told how she had forgotten to ask God's blessing before eating her rice, so she had asked the Lord to forgive her and help her remember each time. "And now, He always reminds me," she said.

Another time she declared, "Now I am going to write a letter to my old man back home and tell him how happy I am and urge him to believe, too." A third time she described how she had already been talking to a neighbor's servant and teaching her. This servant in turn told her mistress that she wanted to believe Jesus, but the mistress had scornfully replied, "What do you know? You can't read."

---

* Mistress

"No," was the answer, "but knowing how to read is not necessary, for the Bible says, 'If you believe in your heart, you will be saved.'"

"And I told her," Old-High continued, "'Don't listen to what people say; just listen to what God says. It doesn't matter if they laugh at you; it only matters if God is pleased. You see, we can pray at any time and God always hears, even when we are cooking or washing or sweeping the floor.'"

The clouds in our refugee corner, too, have been cleared away, and darkness has turned to light. The servants are so eager to read the Bible they get up at daybreak and call us to prayer. They can read their phonetic Bibles; when they come across some wonderful new thought, their faces light up and they catch their breath with joy. Each morning they meet Old-High at the market place, and talk about the Lord to those they meet.

But even this was not the end of Class-Leader's parting bequest. She, being dead, continued to speak: Shining-Virtue, an elder widowed cousin who had been living with Eighth-Brother for many years, and who had also refused to believe all the while, had been deeply impressed by these events. Since she was educated, she now began reading the Bible at last, and in so doing found the Lord and sought to be baptized.

Easter came and among the crowd of war-refugees that filled the makeshift chapel (the beautiful church had been bombed) were Shining-Virtue and these three women servants to be baptized; Ever-Famous and Ever-Wise received communion, and Ever-Cheer and Bright-Cloud's two little daughters were dedicated to the Lord.

So, likewise with me, it has not been easy to be called away from active work and to lie sick in a darkened room for over twenty years; but I always try to remember that even when I cannot see the light, behind the dark clouds the bright sun still shines.

CHAPTER XX

Shades of the Prison House

*P*ROOFREADING for the phonetic required endless hours of eye-taxing concentration; promotion required patient, persistent work as well. Since she could not go out, Miss Leaman had to use every opportunity to interest those who came to see her; the ever-increasing number of callers indicated the appreciation people had for her work. No matter how tired she was, her rule was that no caller be slighted or hurried. In many ways she is more Chinese than the Chinese, in her correct tones and idiomatic language, in her Chinese clothes, and in her Chinese ways. When guests came at mealtime, meals were postponed, or they were invited to share her simple Chinese food. Sometimes when Old-Salt, our cook, put down covered dishes of food in the center of the table, and a bowl of rice before each person, Miss Leaman was too engrossed in her discussion of the phonetic to notice the food or take off the covers, until the poor guest was halfway through the dry rice. Old-Salt, though she worried inwardly, did not make such a breach of etiquette as to suggest to her mistress that the covers come off.

Early in 1941, just before the last chapters of Revelation were finished, Miss Leaman's sight gave out, and it was not easy to do the proofreading of the last sheets. Furthermore, it was not till later that she finally persuaded the Bible Societies to bind the separate books together, and sell the Phonetic Bible as a whole. Only when this was done did she feel her work was accomplished, and then it was too late to take the last evacuation ship to America.

Soon after the Phonetic Bible was completed, came Pearl Harbor, and the Japanese took over the Shanghai concessions. For a year, however, the "belligerent aliens" (as the Japanese called those whose countries were at war with Japan) were given partial freedom to go around the city, but they could not return to America with those from the interior of China, who were sent on the first exchange ship in June, 1942.

In 1943, concentration camps were set up in a number of places, and the "belligerent aliens" were herded into these camps, but the aged and the sick were given another year of grace. So Miss Leaman did not receive the summons to go into camp until June, 1944. Though we tried to keep this fact from being known, so we could have opportunity in the allotted five days to make preparations, all of our friends heard about it; in the last few days while I tried desperately to have all the things packed which she needed, the guests poured in, forty and fifty a day, to express their sympathy. Miss Leaman never once suggested to anyone that she was too tired or too busy to talk to them.

The night before she left, it was one o'clock when the last guest departed, and she came into my room to have prayer. Little-Field, our servant, who was incredibly stupid but devoted to her, broke the key in the lock of my room, and another hour was spent trying to open the door.

Early the next morning guests began to arrive again, and her room was soon crowded. Late in the morning a relative and friend of mine, Mrs. Ling, came to call on me. She was a granddaughter of the Magistrate Ling who burned the British cargo of opium at Canton, in 1830, and so precipitated the Opium War. I had known her from childhood when we studied Buddhism together, and now she was a high-ranking Buddhist. While I often urged her to become a Christian, she tried to persuade me to return to Buddhism. She had a quilt over which hundreds of famous monks had read thousands of prayers, and which she kept to cover her in her coffin when she died, believing it would be efficacious for her in the next incarnation. She had several rosaries, all highly polished, that represented hundreds of thousands of her own prayers as well, so in Buddhist circles her virtue was supreme. When she entered my room she noticed all the callers thronging Miss Leaman's room, so she said to me in surprise, "What is all this about?" I told her that Miss Leaman had to go to concentration camp that very noon, and she was shocked.

The day was unusually hot, and at noontime about fifty friends had gathered at the gate to say good-by to Miss Leaman. She came smilingly to my room, and after prayer she said good-by to me. After the noisy sounds of the rickshas and bicycles had ceased, Mrs. Ling kept on exclaiming, "Not to cry! Not to faint! Just a smile and a prayer! And she's going to prison! I never saw anything like it!" Then she stood up and turned to a Chinese friend from her native city of Foochow, a Miss Lake, who was with us and said, "What religion is this that gives such power to Miss Leaman and Miss Tsai, to enable them to smile under such conditions? Is it possible for me to believe Jesus just in my heart?"

Miss Lake answered, "You ask Miss Tsai about it."

I explained Romans 10: 9, 10, to her: "If thou shalt confess with thy mouth the Lord Jesus, and believe in thine heart that God raised him from the dead, thou shalt be saved." Mrs. Ling said nothing at the time, but she seemed to be thinking it over. A couple of hours later other friends returned saying they had seen Miss Leaman enter a truck that was waiting to take the prisoners to camp. Hardly had these friends seated themselves when Mrs. Ling rose from her chair, and said: "Friends, if Jesus gives such power, I am going to give up Buddhism and accept Jesus as my Saviour." We hardly knew whether to take this announcement as a real confession or not, so said little in answer.

For a month I did not hear further from her, and in the meantime I had moved to another place, so I asked Miss Lake to call on Mrs. Ling and find out what she meant by her statement that day. Mrs. Ling said, "I have been trying all month to get the chief monk here in Shanghai to take my name off the Buddhist membership register, but he refuses to do so. We have been arguing back and

The concentration camp

forth all this time. As soon as this is done I am going to join the Christian Church."

Five months after Miss Leaman went to camp, Mrs. Ling was baptized, joined the church and became a regular attendant. One day she fell and broke her leg, but instead of complaining, she said sweetly, "Maybe the Lord doesn't want so much activity, and would rather I spent the time in bed reading my Bible."

The Lincoln Road Concentration Camp where the Japanese imprisoned about two hundred and fifty of the sick and aged for fourteen months, was the last word in cruelty and deceit. The authorities had promised that there would be full medical care, but when the internees entered the gates of the compound, there was nothing but an empty yard, empty houses and cruel soldiers. Some of the internees came on stretchers, some on crutches, some with open sores, some blind, some tottering on canes, some bowed with pain and suffering. They were assigned to dormitories without discrimination, the crippled to take care of the helpless, and the aged to take care of the bedridden, with only the bed and belongings they themselves had brought along. No medicine, no nurses and no doctors! After three days three prisoners had died, and many more died later. In fact, they would all have died but for fifty able-bodied young people from the other camps, who volunteered to do the hard work and care for these pitiful cases. Different nationalities and religions, hardened sinners and gamblers, the profane and worldly, missionaries and scoffers, rich and poor, senile and children, were all herded together, and in the face of stark reality all masks were off. The selfish became more selfish, the unselfish literally killed themselves serving the others, the complainers complained, the profane swore, the gamblers gambled. But they pooled their strength for the common tasks they were required to do, and shared their medicines; doctors and nurses among them cared for the extreme cases. A diet of poor fish and rice sweepings from the floors of the warehouses started many cases of dysentery, and the swarming mosquitoes brought malaria. Miss Leaman, who had gamblers at her side playing cards much of the time, sat in her bed and peeled potatoes, or cleaned the dirty rice. Of course, she shared some of the food I sent her and did what she could to help others, but she was taken sick with dysentery and malaria and lost forty pounds in fourteen months; her spinal curvature got so much worse she lost five inches in height.

As for me, I had almost no money, and our servants were all gone. Old-Salt died, Little-King went home to her only son who was dying, and Little-Field went to her mother-in-law. I rented an attic room in an old house in Brown-Family-Gardens. This I kept dark, since I could not bear the light, and as I could not walk, I learned to crawl on the floor whenever I had to move around. A Christian teacher next door got me a warm meal once a day when she came home at night, and the rest of the time I lived on hard biscuits and salted vegetables.

Many a time I said to the Lord, "The way is too narrow, I cannot pass through"; but He always answered, "Hide in Me and I will take you through." A friend saw my straits and found a unique way to help me. Some Buddhist nuns were also in great need, and one of them, a Mrs. Temple, agreed to make a Buddhist bargain with me. She promised to help me in this life, if I promised to help her in the next life. She faithfully carried out her part, helping me cook and keeping me company, and we became good friends. She and I sat in the dark room together, she counting her beads and I at my devotions. But she was willing to learn to sing hymns and read the Bible and pray with me. At the end of the year she and her daughter accepted Christ and He made them His children for eternity. So I was able to carry out my part of the bargain.

Some foreign friends had agreed to send Miss Leaman a package each month, but they soon came over and said they had no money to do it. I had only two small cans of fruit and some charcoal to send her that month. Nourishing food that would not spoil was almost unprocurable in Shanghai. As bank accounts were frozen, I sold everything I had and then borrowed money at exorbitant rates to get her wheat biscuits, dates, peanut butter and other things. As for milk, it had to be bought at the black market and carried out of the shop one little tin at a time, carefully hidden in the clothing. It was Miss Lake and others who searched the shops to find things for me.

There was a general report going around that the Japanese were trying to starve the internees, and one morning I prayed for a five-pound tin of powdered milk to send Miss Leaman. A couple of hours later, our friend Spring-Hill sent me a telephone message saying, "Brother Willow, a rich merchant, had hoarded three five-pound tins of powdered milk, but when he went to church on Sunday the preacher said anyone who doesn't give his tenth or help God's needy children is stealing from the Lord. So Brother Willow asked me to take one of the tins over to you to send to Miss Leaman."

You can imagine how my burden was lifted and how my faith was strengthened! It was a Godsend, because I couldn't have gotten it otherwise at any price. These packages saved her life and those of others as well, but they and other expenses put me in debt three thousand U.S. dollars.

V-J day came at last, and Chinese friends flocked to the concentration camps with food and gifts. One man had hidden some coffee and canned milk, and now he opened a stall offering the internees all the coffee they could drink, free of charge. A woman brought roast chicken and baked potatoes for them. The Generalissimo and Madam Chiang gave each one a gift of money, and others found different ways to help them. Since I could not ride alone, a woman doctor went with me in a ricksha to see Miss Leaman. I was shocked to see how thin and short she had become. She told me she had been forbidden by the American authorities to leave the camp for one month and that she had to return to America as the doctors had examined her spine and told her she must avoid any lifting or jolting, for fear her spine would break.

When I returned home I had a long string of callers who kept me up till two o'clock in the morning, and the next day there were many more. The result was that I woke on the morning of the third day shaking violently all over. The nun held me in her arms, but could not stop the trembling. I finally fell back on the bed unconscious and I remained in that state for four months. Miss Leaman heard of my illness, and happily a way was opened for her to come to see me. One of the American authorities took her to the city in his car, and she went to the American headquarters and asked permission to leave the camp, saying she could not stand going back to camp and that she had a bed and room near at hand. At the end of the day after much pleading the doctor gave her permission to stay for three weeks, and she walked slowly all the way to where I lived, a distance of about a mile. I did not recognize her when she came in, and called her "Big Brother." So here she was with a nearly broken spine, and I unconscious and burning with fever. War, inflation and prison camps had wrought havoc with people's money. She was penniless and I three thousand dollars in debt. But another miracle happened. A friend whom I had met only twice, came in and asked for me. Miss Leaman explained my condition, so he threw a packet on her lap, saying, "I do not need this now. You use it and repay it when convenient."

"What is your name?" Miss Leaman asked. "Don't you want a receipt?"

"Miss Tsai knows me, and I trust her. She is a Christian." Saying this he left. Miss Leaman opened the package, and it contained three thousand one hundred dollars in U.S. money. Food, medicine and servants could be procured once more, the debts gradually repaid. Where there was life there was hope!

CHAPTER XXI

Just a Hunting Dog

MISS LEAMAN sent for our old servants, Little-King and Little-Field, and obtained for me all the medical care that was available. But for a year and a half I lingered on, unconscious much of the time, for the fever in my bones could not be stopped. Doctors now diagnosed the trouble as a combination of pellagra, dysentery and malignant malaria. The reason why malaria had not been discovered earlier was that the parasites were in the bones and in the brain cells, not in the blood stream. Dysentery and malaria are of many varieties and I had several kinds of them. Only one medicine of the many new remedies was able to stop the fever, and that was Aralen. The story of how we got it was another miracle.

One day Dr. Mandel came and examined me. He told Miss Leaman, "If it were anyone else but Miss Tsai, I would say that within three days she would die. But I can't be sure, and our only hope is to find some way of stopping the fever." Miss Leaman told him that a Chinese friend, Mr. Grass-Head, was interested in my case. He had seen a bottle of a new medicine for malaria which had just been brought over from America, and had told the owner not to sell it until we had a chance to buy it. However, she did not know Mr. Grass-Head's address and had no way of finding him.

After the doctor left, it suddenly came to her that before she went into the concentration camp, Mr. Grass-Head had given her his address to take with her, in case she was repatriated; for safety's sake, lest the Japanese get hold of it, she had written it scattered through the leaves of her Bible. When she found it, she called him up and asked him to get the medicine right away and take it to Dr. Mandel. Then she called Dr. Mandel and asked him to stay at home till Mr. Grass-Head arrived. While Dr. Mandel was waiting, his wife showed him an article in a magazine describing a new remedy for malaria. As he was reading it, Mr. Grass-Head arrived and this proved to be the same medicine, Aralen, described in the article. As far as we know, it was the only bottle to be found in Shanghai. The Aralen soon brought down my fever; the crisis passed, I regained consciousness, and once more emerged out of the valley of the shadow of death. Though I improved, I have never been able to walk alone, or to bear the light. Until God performs another miracle, these chronic diseases can only be alleviated; there is no human cure as yet.

How Miss Leaman carried on during this time is another epic of faith and will power, for she had to spend most of the time in bed. Her attic room next to mine was furnished with only a bed, a table and a few straight chairs, while reconstructed packing-cases and makeshift shelves lined the walls. Half of the room was curtained off for the servants and the stores of food. We had a second white Persian cat which invariably stayed beside her. On one side of the bed was a packing-case table on which were a telephone, bottles of medicine and an electric hot plate; a typewriter, Phonetic Bible, address book and other things were on the bed, or underneath, so she could reach them without getting up.

From morning until late at night she was busy. Our electric fixtures were invariably breaking down, and the electrician had to be coaxed every day to send his apprentice to tinker with them. The manservant would come in with the marketing and Miss Leaman had to check accounts with him, plan the meals, and dole out the supplies of rice and oil. Mr. Season, a refugee pastor and amateur carpenter, was often there hammering new shelves and packing-case furniture. The tenants downstairs and neighbors next door spent hours every day airing their problems with her. The hypos had to be sterilized, the doctor assisted, and medicines administered, and everyone fed at different times. The busy servants had to be caught one by one and encouraged to read the Bible and pray. Students of the phonetic were often working with her in the room. Besides, she had to answer the telephone, which was the only one in the house, and send for the person wanted.

All the while these other things were going on, there was a steady stream of callers coming and going; or they sat around, singly or in groups, waiting their turn. Each of these had to be entertained for a few minutes, or a few hours, as they chose; before they left she always prayed with them. Her guests included business-men, refugees, missionaries from the interior, old Chinese friends, neighbors in trouble, newcomers to Shanghai, teachers and students from all over China. She welcomed all and with every opportunity she explained the importance of the phonetic. At night when she had to do her writing, often the telephone would ring. Some lonely foreigner in Shanghai, who wanted a friendly chat, had mistaken her number in the telephone book. She faithfully told them God's way to satisfy lonely hearts and influenced several to go to church.

During my illness Sixth Brother came to see me frequently. All these years he and his family had persistently refused to accept the Lord, but now he was moved at my suffering. One day, un-known to me and on his own initiative, he called the members of our family together. They gathered, wondering what he had to say; but he soon told them. "I have an announcement to make to you," he said. "I have been to see Seventh Sister many times and wondered how she could endure all this suffering. Now I can see that she has been given some sustaining power and can only explain it as coming from God. So I have decided there must be a God after all. I have read the Bible and realize that I am a sinner. So here and now I want to tell you that I have accepted Christ as my Saviour, asked Him to forgive my sins, and promised to follow Him."

So the brother who tore up my Bible and persecuted me in the early days, at last confessed my Lord. In all, fifty-five of my relatives, adults and children, have become God's children and expressed their faith in Jesus. I have never been to college, or theological seminary, and I am not a Bible teacher; I have only been God's "hunting dog." I simply followed at the heels of my Master, and brought to His feet the quarry He sent me after.

CHAPTER XXII

From Shanghai to Paradise

D URING 1947 and 1948 two Chinese doctors, Dr. and Mrs. Martial, lived near us at Brown-Family-Gardens, and they gave me injections and medical treatment. They were a young couple, both atheists, but they were skillful and kind, and I owe them a great deal. I am thankful to say that after two years, on Christmas Eve, the wife openly confessed the Lord Jesus, and her husband was later influenced to follow. They and many other friends urged us to leave Shanghai, because they said I could never get well in that malarial climate.

You can imagine how questions thundered in my mind like the rolling waves of the sea. How could we ever climb up and down that steep gangway to the steamer? How could we invalids travel halfway around the world? How could I ever stand the light and sounds again after being in a quiet, darkened room so long? Who was going to hand me the many things I needed during the day? How could I ever manage to enter into entirely different surroundings after being shut in for eighteen years with my loyal but ignorant country women who cared for me so patiently day after day and night after night, like a mother would care for a sick child? How could I suddenly leave my loved ones, friends, doctors, servants and also our phonetic work for the millions of illiterates of China? There seemed no end to such questions.

One day we thought we had better go to Hongkong; the next we planned to go to Manila; the third day we decided to stay in Shanghai; and the fourth, fifth and sixth days we had other ideas!

Early one morning, the words of Mrs. George Fitch, a missionary of great influence in Shanghai in the early years, brought rest to my soul:

"Say then to thy troubled soul, 'Rest thyself in His control, not just the part, but rest the whole.'"

Three nights in succession the Lord said to me, "Daughter, thy faith hath saved thee; go in peace." At last, about daybreak, I took up my telephone and told Miss Leaman that the Lord had told me to go to the United States, and that I was ready to go.

She answered, "I have applied for reservations, but there is no space on the ships. I have been told that there are three hundred on the waiting list." However, three or four hours after this, the morning mail brought a letter from the President Lines telling us they had a room for us, and that the "President Wilson" was to sail in a week! Dr. Martial left his other work for the day to take us to the ship, and two other friends, Dr. Thorngate and his son, carried me the whole length of the dock. Five more friends, and three weeping servants, accompanied us. All of them pushed and pulled and half carried us up the steep gangway, and took us to our quiet little cabin. So, on January 18, 1949, the "President Wilson" took us across the Pacific Ocean away from our dear old China. The Lord's provision all along the journey was wonderful. The stewardess and the room boy could not have been better. When the time came to go on deck, I did not dare lean on Miss Leaman, for fear of hurting her back; the Lord provided a friend just at the right moment.

On the third of Febuary, long before sunrise, our boat moved slowly through the Golden Gate into the Bay of San Francisco. We were met by Miss Lorna Logan and Miss Tien-fu-Wu, and received many telegrams and airmail letters of welcome. There was a taxi strike on in San Francisco when we landed, but two private cars were loaned for our use. The next day Miss Logan and Miss Wu drove us across the lovely Bay bridge to Oakland, where a red cap with a wheel chair awaited us and took us to a little compartment on the transcontinental express to New York. Here the porter proved very kind and thoughtful. Because of unusually heavy snows, our train was delayed, and we spent four days and nights in our compartment. The delay disrupted our schedule and sister Lucy's as well, so the porter suggested that we telegraph for wheel chairs to meet us at Lancaster, Pennsylvania, our destination. Though it was four-thirty on a cold, dark winter morning when our train made a special stop at Lancaster, we found two men with wheel chairs waiting for us on the platform!

Our hearts beat fast as we drew near home. Nothing was ever more beautiful than the lights of home, and nothing warmer than the welcome that awaited us. The whole house was lighted, and sister Lucy and cousin Mary were standing at the door looking for us. It seemed as if I were transported to Heaven. I thought of the last Home-going the wonderful lights up there and the Father waiting for us with His welcome smiles, and my heart was thrilled. All I can now say is, "The Lord led us all the way from faraway Shanghai to Paradise,* to the beautiful old home belonging to my godmother, Mary Leaman, her sister Lucy, and cousin Mary. I am deeply grateful that they have given me such a happy shelter and quiet security." And now from my home in Paradise I want to add a few lines to this story.

When we went away from Shanghai we had to leave behind all the matrices, type and papier mâché shells needed for reprinting the Phonetic Bible, and though various efforts have been made to have them shipped out, all have been futile. But for a providential encounter and a bit of foresight on Miss Leaman's part there would now be no chance to restock the already depleted supply of Phonetic Bibles. But God, who sees the end from the beginning, provided for that emergency.

A short time before Pearl Harbor the work of preparing the Phonetic Bible was completed, and the printer who had successfully bid for the job unexpectedly came to tell Miss Leaman that the presses were ready to begin printing. Of course she was delighted, but foresaw a disastrous eventuality. What if America should be

---

*Paradise is the name of the town where the Leaman home is located.

drawn into war with Japan? Such a possibility could spell the ruin of this great task.

"Before you print the Bible," she said, "I think it would be a good idea to buy the best white paper you can procure in Shanghai, and run off ten sets using only one side of each sheet. We can keep those sets for lithographic reprints if we should lose our matrices and papier-mâché shells."

"Oh, Miss Leaman," the printer exclaimed, "good paper is too expensive under these war conditions. We can't afford it. You couldn't get that done for less than three hundred American dollars!"

"God will provide the money," she said; "you do it."

So it came to pass that he brought her ten sets on fine white paper as soon as he could and she cached them in different places—one in the Swiss Consulate, one in the Hongkong and Shanghai Bank, one in the loft in a German friend's home. Soon after this came Pearl Harbor, so it was not till after the war was over and she was released from concentration camp, that she could send for her cached Bibles. Only three sets were intact, and these sets we brought with us when we came to the United States.

Now there is a need for a new edition to teach the standard Pekinese to the many thousand overseas Chinese who speak Amoy or Cantonese and whose children know no Chinese at all. The American Bible Society wrote us that they have requests for the Phonetic Bible, but have none in stock; they asked if there is any way to make a reprint. You can imagine our joy and thankfulness to tell them of these sets and to urge them to print a new edition.

We have received encouraging news of the work of the Phonetic being carried on in Formosa as well. I quote from a letter written by Mrs. Twinem:

My dear friends C.T. and M.L.,

I am enclosing a book to show you that no prayers and no letters of entreaty are needed now for pushing the work of the phonetic on this island. It is used universally on street signs, newspapers, etc.

Lovingly,
M.F.T.

There is a laymen's movement going on among the Chinese over there called the Gospel Jacket Crusade. It started some years ago with a stuttering Christian who was burning with zeal for the Saviour. He wanted to witness for Christ, but he had difficulty. Determined not to be silenced, he found two pieces of cardboard on which he wrote in large characters, "Good works will not save you," and "Believe on the Lord Jesus and be saved." These he hung, one in front and one behind like a sandwich man and walked slowly from one street to another. First one person and then another came up to read the words and he was soon accompanied by a crowd of men, women and children.

The interest aroused was so inspiring that soon other would-be witnesses followed his example, but they wrote verses on squares of white cloth which they sewed to their clothes. From city to city and town to town the movement spread; the white cloth squares were replaced by white sleeveless jackets, and the Christians started going together in bands, blowing trumpets and singing hymns. When they had collected a good crowd in some open space, they stopped and one of the number started to preach. As a result of this spontaneous gospel jacket crusade, many Christians have found they can witness, and thousands of listeners have confessed their sins and accepted Christ.

Just as I thought my story was closed, I received a letter from my niece, Bright-Cloud, which brought me both grief and comfort. It told news of my nephew, Ping-ping. As I read this I recalled the last time I had seen him. I was sick in Shanghai, and the doctor had said I might die at any time, and Ping-ping had brought his bride to my bedside. He held my hand, and could only say in a choked voice, "Seventh-Auntie." I was touched by his affection, and answered in a whisper, "Ping-ping, whatever happens, trust in Jesus. He will comfort you and give you peace." The servants who accompanied them out later told me what they said as they left.

"Do you know Jesus?" Ping-ping asked his bride.

"No," she answered; "this is the first time I ever heard the name. But Seventh-Auntie must know Him very well since in her illness she could say, 'Whatever happens trust in Jesus. He will comfort you and give you peace'!" So the words in Bright-Cloud's letter that brought me comfort and grief were these:

> Ping-ping has been killed, leaving his wife and little daughter.
> But his wife has found comfort and peace in Jesus and has joined the church.

I have indeed found peace out of pain, joy in suffering, light in darkness; after over twenty-years in bed, I can say it is worth while to pass through the valley of the shadow of death for the joy of knowing the Lord Jesus Christ.

I want to finish this testimony by quoting from a poem. This poem sums up the past, present and future in words that express my own thankfulness and trust.

> O fathomless mercy! O infinite grace!
> With humble thanksgiving the road I retrace.
> Thou never hast failed me, my Strength and my Stay!
> To whom should I turn for the rest of the way?

> Through dangers, through darkness, by day and by night,
> Thou ever hast guided and guided aright:
> In Thee have I trusted and peacefully lay
> My hand in Thy hand for the rest of the way.

> Thy cross all my refuge, Thy blood all my plea,
> None other I need, blessed Jesus but Thee!
> I fear not the shadows at close of life's day,
> For Thou wilt go with me the rest of the way.

Queen of the

Dark Chamber

Waiting for

Her

King of Light